L E E D S
U N I T E D

The Return to Glory

Ian Ross

MAINSTREAM
PUBLISHING

EDINBURGH AND LONDON

ACKNOWLEDGMENT

Special thanks to Gary McAllister – a great footballer and a perceptive observer

First published in Great Britain in 1992 by
MAINSTREAM PUBLISHING COMPANY (EDINBURGH) LTD
7 Albany Street
Edinburgh EH1 3UG

ISBN 1 85158 508 7

A catalogue record for this book is available from the British Library

Typeset in Impressum by Saxon Printing Ltd, Derby

Printed in Great Britain by Billings & Sons Ltd, Worcester

CONTENTS

Dedicated to Jennifer Laura Ross,
my best friend

Chapter One

THE WAY WE WERE

There is more than a touch of irony to the fact that a very high percentage of those supporters of Leeds United who rose to salute the club's League Championship success at the end of the 1991-92 season will have done so to mark a beginning rather than the resumption of a service which was once regarded as normal but which latterly appeared to have been discontinued.

For those supporters born after, say, 1970, meandering and lavishly embroidered tales of titles, FA Cups and European trophies were mentally catalogued along with the fanciful outpourings of Enid Blyton and Roald Dahl; they were fairy stories and folklore handed down by possibly aging relatives who could recall in great detail the "good old days" but who preferred Jimmy Hill to Jonathon Ross and Thunderbirds to the Teenage Mutant Hero Turtles.

One of the prerequisites of youth is an ability to disregard totally what has gone before and to live for the moment. The generations of the Seventies and Eighties will lovingly embrace junk food, junk television – and even junk football – but, with typical impatience, they will reject the suggestion that to enjoy the present you must in some way be respectful of the past.

It is, perhaps, an opportune moment to reflect on that past, a mind-numbing rise from obscurity to prominence which was followed by a painful decline.

As Leslie Silver, the Leeds chairman, has stressed on numerous occasions in recent months, before Don Revie

and the startling metamorphosis which he single-hand-
edly prompted, Leeds United was a club without any
discernible tradition. After rising from the ashes of the
disgraced Leeds City who had been expelled from the
Football League in 1919 after a scandal involving alleged
illegal payments to players during the First World War,
Leeds United was, to all intents and purposes, the
archetypal yo-yo club, moving between the top two
divisions with bewildering rapidity.

When, in 1961, the Leeds board dispensed with the
services of Jack Taylor and installed Revie as team
manager, Leeds was a Second Division club of dubious
pedigree. Indeed, had the final game of the season
against Newcastle United at St James Park not ended in
victory, relegation would have been confirmed and
Revie's improbable revolution would quite possibly
never have happened.

With his club in debt to the tune of £100,000, Revie was
required to use his considerable business acumen as he
sought to build a side capable of winning promotion.
With the accent firmly on youth, Leeds began to build and
began to prosper.

A 2–0 win over Charlton on the final day of the 1963–64
season clinched the Second Division Championship for a
team which was littered with largely unknown players,
among them Gary Sprake, Paul Reaney, Jack Charlton,
Norman Hunter, Billy Bremner, Bobby Collins and
Johnny Giles. Rather like Howard Wilkinson's side,
Revie's men were not expected to make any significant
impression upon their return to the First Division but, by
January of the following season, Leeds United were at
the top of English football for the first time in their
history.

Leeds had extended their unbeaten League and cup
run to 25 games when they were finally defeated by their
nearest rivals – Manchester United – at Elland Road in
mid-April. It was a defeat which was to eventually cost
them the Championship.

Having lost the title on goal average (the forerunner of
goal difference), Leeds endured yet more heartbreak
when they were beaten by Liverpool in the FA Cup final,

2–1 after extra time. They didn't know it at the time but disappointment was to become a way of life in the years which lay ahead.

Between 1965 and 1968 Leeds were never to finish outside of the top four but, despite enjoying a reputation for collective ruthlessness and unparalleled professionalism, the big prize, the Football League Championship, was to elude them.

Having gained a tangible reward for some breathtaking football by winning the League Cup in 1968, Leeds were to be finally crowned as worthy Champions in 1969 when they lost just two of their 42 League fixtures. Just as in 1991–92, it was Leeds' surprise elimination from the major knock-out competitions which was to precipitate Championship success.

In the following season, 1969-70, Leeds launched a sustained bid to land what would have been a unique treble of League Championship, FA Cup and European Cup. It was to end in glorious failure. As the pressure of playing two games every week began to mount, the title was surrendered to Everton, the FA Cup was lost to Chelsea in a replay at Old Trafford and the pursuit of European Football's top honour ended in semi-final defeat by Glasgow Celtic.

Leeds were again Championship runners-up in 1970-71 but they did win the Inter Cities Fairs Cup for a second time by defeating mighty Juventus of Italy on the away goals ruling.

Although the following season was to again bring disappointment on the league front, it was to yield the FA Cup for the only time in the club's history – Allan Clarke's famous diving header finally putting paid to Arsenal at Wembley.

Twelve months later, Revie's side was back beneath the twin towers seeking to retain the trophy only to be denied by Second Division Sunderland. Eleven days after that embarrassment, AC Milan compounded Leeds' misery by winning the European Cup Winners Cup in controversial circumstances.

Rather fittingly, Revie's last season at the helm – 1973-74 – was to end with the club recapturing the

League Championship. It was a success which was to mark the end of a golden era and the opening of an extended period which is now popularly referred to as "the dark days".

The man chosen to follow Revie was Brian Clough, a manager of proven ability but one who had constantly criticised Leeds for the robust nature of their football. He swiftly set about dismantling his predecessor's squad, but amid allegations of "player-power" he was dismissed after just 44 days.

Next up was Jimmy Armfield, the amiable and articulate former England international. The highlight of his four-year reign came in his first season when he led Leeds through into the final of the European Cup only for rioting supporters to make even more miserable a 2–0 defeat by Bayern Munich. Although Armfield took his side to the semi-finals of both the FA and League Cups, the Leeds board was growing impatient and he was dismissed to be replaced by Jock Stein. After emulating Brian Clough by spending exactly 44 days at Elland Road, Stein walked out to take up the chance to manage the Scotland national side.

Jimmy Adamson was the next man to boldly place his reputation on the line and, for a time, he appeared to be on the verge of dragging a faltering club back on to the straight and narrow. Adamson, who had once rejected the opportunity to become the manager of England, took Leeds to fifth place in Division One at the end of his first season – the best since the departure of Revie. His joy was, however, short-lived. In March 1980, mounted police were summoned to Elland Road to break up an angry demonstration by an increasingly disgruntled support. Seven months later, Adamson bowed to the inevitable and tendered his resignation.

It was at this point that the Leeds board attempted to move forward by glancing back over their shoulders to gaze affectionately at the not-too-distant past. Allan Clarke, the prince of goal-scorers, was lured from Barnsley, where he had enjoyed enormous success, and told to recapture the spirit of the glory days which he himself had helped to fashion. The logic was simple – if

Liverpool could build an empire with the help of former players then so could Leeds. It didn't work.

Clarke thought big – "We will win the European Cup within a matter of a few years" – but sadly his inexperience was amply illustrated by his decision to pay a club record fee of £980,000 for Peter Barnes, a gifted player who contributed little or nothing to the Leeds cause. Clarke's dismissal in 1982 following Leeds' relegation was hardly a surprise.

Eddie Gray, one of the finest footballers of his generation, was in charge between 1982 and 1985 but despite enjoying limited success he too was shown the door. The end of Gray's 22-year association with the club was not well received on the terraces or in the dressing-room. Indeed, Peter Lorimer, the club captain at the time, handed in a letter to the board in which the players condemned the timing and handling of the announcement.

As a player, Billy Bremner had led Leeds to their greatest triumphs but his determined attempts to rekindle success from behind the managerial desk were to end in failure. Leeds were languishing near the foot of the Second Division table when Bremner was called into a board meeting in October 1988, and informed that his contract had been cancelled with immediate effect.

"It was pretty obvious what Leeds were trying to do around this time – they were trying to copy the Liverpool method of natural progression," says Terry Yorath, once a mainstay of the Leeds midfield, now the manager of Wales.

"The idea was a good one but the problem was that successive managers were not given sufficient financial backing. It was no good the board turning around and saying that Don Revie's team had been home-grown because that collection of players was a one-off; a once in a lifetime thing.

"There are very many reasons why Leeds United went into decline. Quite possibly the experienced players stayed at the club for too long, so restricting the progress of the youngsters within the first-team squad. I don't think the choice of manager was always right, to be honest.

"Actually, Jimmy Armfield was one of the best managers the club ever had. Perhaps they should have stuck with him for a little bit longer. I couldn't ever see things working out for Brian Clough. There was a great deal of animosity between him and those players he inherited, simply because he had been so scathing about them in the past.

"Whenever you talk about Brian Clough you have to think carefully about what might have been because he went on to enjoy tremendous success after leaving Elland Road.

"Clarke, Gray and Bremner all worked their socks off in an attempt to rediscover a winning formula but, sadly, it was not to be. The club was ready for something new – something fresh – after Billy had been sacked. It was crying out for a new broom to sweep it clean. As it turns out, it was crying out for a man like Howard Wilkinson," he added.

Chapter Two

MARCHING ON TOGETHER

On 27 April 1992, as Elland Road and all things Leeds United were being enveloped by a positive tidal wave of euphoria, one man sat quietly in his office, enjoying the relative tranquillity afforded by a few precious moments alone.

Twenty-four hours earlier the impossible dream had become pleasant reality. Leeds' defeat of Yorkshire rivals Sheffield United at Bramall Lane coupled with Liverpool's emphatic triumph over Manchester United at Anfield had finally shaped the outcome of one of the most intriguing – and unpredictable – League Championship duels for many years. After an agonising wait of 18 years, Leeds United were once again champions; once again perched at the very summit of English football. It was not an event which the club's millions of followers the world over were about to let pass by unheralded.

As players drifted in and out of the stadium, drawn not by a sense of duty but by a sense of genuine occasion, the telephones started to ring – they didn't stop for days. Telegrams, postcards, letters, flowers and gifts flowed into the Elland Road reception area. Supporters, proudly wearing the hats and scarves handed down within families for generations, filled the concourse outside the main entrance. History had been made and it seemed that everyone wanted to play at least a supporting role.

Upstairs, Leslie Silver, the club's chairman and visionary force, possibly allowed himself a wry smile of satisfaction as he recalled the events of a day, three and a half

11

years earlier, which had, in effect, shaped the destiny of the club he adores. His own significant, perhaps overlooked, contribution to a remarkable story of transformation and subsequent success had been made on a wintry afternoon back in October 1988.

On that day, Leeds, once the powerful overlords of English football, the aristocratic masters of the professional game, were down on their luck, sinking with uncommon and unacceptable speed and most definitely in need of salvation. Although the 1987-88 season was still very much in its infancy, the prospect of ignominious relegation to the Third Division was already a distinct possibility. The team had slipped perilously close to the bottom of the Second Division and, with player morale disintegrating swiftly, Silver convened the club's board of directors for an emergency meeting.

The major topic of discussion – if not the only topic of discussion – was how to arrest a slide in fortune which was blighting the club's immediate and long-term future. By its very nature, football in this country can be a cruel and heartless sport. The buck stops at the manager's office; it never travels any further. Billy Bremner was one of Leeds United's favoured sons. A magnificent player and captain, he had led the club to glory during the unforgettable Revie era. He was a hero – but he was also the man charged with responsibility for team affairs. Leeds United's progress had stopped, and so had the buck.

At the conclusion of the meeting it was decided that Bremner's three-year reign was at an end, whether he liked it or not. The diminutive Scotsman was duly informed and in a simple public announcement it was stated that the two parties had gone their separate ways and it was hoped the club would be in a position to announce a successor in the not too distant future.

After failing in an audacious, bold bid to persuade Howard Kendall to resign his post with the leading Spanish First Division club, Athletic Bilbao, Silver set his sights on Howard Wilkinson.

Wilkinson, Yorkshire-born and with a reputation for putting dissenters firmly in their place with one, well-chosen acidic comment, was in charge at Sheffield Wednesday, having moved to Hillsborough in 1983 after a brief, but nonetheless highly successful, spell at Notts County. After several years in the wilderness, Wednesday were faring well under Wilkinson's leadership. His ability to plunder the transfer market for low-priced players of quality and experience had helped to lift the club into a healthy position in the First Division. The club's supporters had accepted the introduction of football loosely based on the often-reviled long-ball system without so much as a murmur of discontent and with his board promising more money for squad-strengthening, things were looking bright.

The task of persuading Wilkinson to leave a club which appeared to be on the very threshold of success and to move to one which was enduring one of the least productive and traumatic spells in its long history was not going to be an easy one.

Undeterred by the prospect of failure, Silver and his team moved in. Wilkinson was approached and invited to travel the 35 miles which separates the two clubs to discuss the possibility of him filling the chair recently vacated by Bremner.

Quite possibly out of nothing more than curiosity, Wilkinson agreed to travel and meet up with the silver-tongued Silver. Later that day, in a move which was greeted with widespread surprise (and possibly disgust in Sheffield itself) Wilkinson was confirmed as Leeds United's eighth manager since Don Revie resigned in 1974 to take over the England national team.

Silver remembers well the day he convinced Howard Wilkinson that his future lay in West, and not South, Yorkshire. "If I was to say that we had to do a real selling job on Howard it would be a gross understatement. When we met up we knew, full well, that everything was stacked against us. Sheffield Wednesday were doing really well at the time. In fact, I think they were in either fifth or sixth place in the First Division table.

"Howard had established himself at Hillsborough. He had assembled a strong first-team squad and he was popular with the club's supporters. There is no doubt at all that his future was bright and so was the future of Sheffield Wednesday.

"I don't suppose that there was any good reason why he should decide to leave there to come here. They were on the up, we weren't; they were in the top flight, we weren't. No, I can't think of a good reason. I knew that the only way to convince him that he should seriously consider the offer we were making was to outline, in detail, exactly what it was we had to offer.

"It took time. He must have been in my office for between five and six hours just sitting there, quietly listening. What we wanted to do, what we were desperate to do, was to convince him that our targets, our ambitions, were both realistic and attainable. There is no point at all in trotting out a list of hopeful future objectives if you do not sincerely believe that you can reach them.

"In the end, we obviously succeeded because he accepted our offer. I was delighted because I thought that we had the best available man for what was obviously a very difficult and demanding job. It is very difficult for me to say exactly where this club would be had we failed. That is, of course, one of life's great imponderables. Would we now be the Football League champions? I honestly don't know. What I do know is that on that day in 1988 we found ourselves a superb manager whose personal ambition matched the ambition of Leeds United Football Club."

Having taken up the reins at Elland Road, Wilkinson's first objective was simple, straightforward in the extreme but so very important – he had to preserve the club's status by banishing the threat of relegation. On paper at least it was an easily obtainable target for a manager of proven ability. However, the burden was increased by the inescapable fact that those players he had inherited were bereft of confidence and lacking in self-belief.

By working swiftly with what he had at his disposal, Wilkinson began to alter the course of a season which at one point had seemed destined to end in abject despair. Like any self-respecting manager, Wilkinson refused to plunge straight into the transfer market to boost his resources. While his board had made it clear that money was readily available, he bided his time and carefully assessed the strengths and weaknesses of his senior panel.

Changes were, of course, inevitable but not until after Leeds' Second Division future had been all but assured did Wilkinson ask for permission to remove cash from the club's coffers. In March 1989, Wilkinson was to spend the grand total of just £800,000 on two men who were to make significant contributions to the great revival. Chris Fairclough, a talented centre-back who had failed to make any real impression at Tottenham Hotspur after a move from his first League club, Nottingham Forest, was bought for £500,000 but, more significantly, Gordon Strachan was purchased from Manchester United for £300,000.

Strachan, the archetypal aggressive Scotsman, had spent five successful years at Old Trafford but as Alex Ferguson attempted to construct a side capable of winning the League Championship for the first time in more than two decades, he had become, to all intents and purposes, surplus to requirements. Strachan, who was still a model of consistency despite having entered what most people assumed to be the twilight of an illustrious career, was immensely popular with the Manchester public and Ferguson's decision to sanction his sale was greeted with unease in some quarters.

Virtually everyone within English football now regards the compact midfielder as the inspirational driving force behind Leeds' dramatic revival and while Ferguson has insisted, on a regular basis, that only by moving away from Old Trafford could he hope to extend his career, he must still rue his decision to do business with a club which was to deny him the ultimate glory at the end of the 1991–92 season.

Rather ironically, Strachan was asked to do what Billy Bremner had done for Leeds in the mid-Sixties, namely run the midfield with authority. It was a job which he approached with enthusiasm and relish.

At the end of a season which was simply about consolidation and survival, Leeds had risen to a position of some respectability in Division Two, a splendid achievement under the circumstances. Having laid the foundation stones, albeit on a bedrock which was still far from stable, Wilkinson began to look to the future.

As he was to publicly admit in the wake of the Championship triumph, his plan was to build a side which would be capable of escaping from the Second Division in the 1990-91 season. For once, the normally accurate Wilkinson got things wrong but few found room for complaint as the Second Division Championship was seized, 12 months ahead of schedule. Wilkinson's policy of introducing new talent when it was most needed was proving to be highly successful and during the 1989–90 season two more crucial signings were made.

In July, 1989, Mel Sterland was lured away from Glasgow Rangers in a £600,000 deal and shortly after the turn of the year, the much-travelled and vastly experienced Lee Chapman was brought in to add firepower to the Leeds attack in a £400,000 deal with Nottingham Forest. Although it has to be said that neither deal sparked mass celebrations on the terraces, both men have proved wrong those critics who vociferously insisted that only by paying inflated prices for talented youngsters whose potential usually far outweighs their actual usefulness can clubs hope to prosper.

A campaign which quite often touched heights of pure excellence and which was always sustained by consistency reached a fitting climax at Bournemouth on the season's final day when Chapman's solitary goal guaranteed promotion. After eight years of Second Division football, eight years of broken promises and squandered opportunity, Leeds United were finally back in the First Division.

Having returned Leeds to the promised land, Wilkinson was faced by a wholly predictable dilemma. Although several of those players who had been instrumental in transforming the club's fortunes were tried, trusted and working efficiently within a régime which demanded professionalism of the very highest order, they were also lacking in experience and possibly ill-equipped to handle the transition from Second to First Division.

Had Wilkinson's ambition embraced nothing grander than mere survival amongst the likes of Liverpool, Arsenal, Everton and Manchester United, he would have been a contented man. The squad which he had at his disposal would almost certainly have negotiated a safe passage through what was certain to be a difficult season. However, Wilkinson's brief upon succeeding Bremner was not to simply win back the place in Division One which had been surrendered back in 1982 but to assemble a side which was capable not only of living with the very best, but of beating the very best on a regular basis.

Money was needed and money was provided. New players were needed and new players were bought. This time the "new boys" did not represent bargain buys nor could they, in any way at all, be described as other people's cast-offs.

Having won a League Championship medal at Arsenal, John Lukic, a goalkeeper of proven ability, returned to Elland Road in a £1 million deal seven years after he had left to join the London club in a deal which had netted Leeds the princely sum of £50,000. Shortly afterwards, Wilkinson beat off the challenge of several leading English and Scottish clubs, notably Nottingham Forest, to secure the services of Gary McAllister, a midfielder of great vision whose ability to pick out a colleague from a distance was second to none. Slowly, subtly the make-up of the Leeds team which Wilkinson had inherited less than two years earlier was beginning to change.

The fact that players of the ability of Lukic and McAllister had chosen to join a club which had, for so long, been forced to live with the tag of "unfashionable" led to a change in attitude, not only in managerial circles but also within the ranks of the influential media.

"Once Howard began to sign quality footballers it became clear – very quickly – that he meant business. He was spending a great deal of money but the important thing was that he was spending it very wisely on men who were very much in demand," says Everton manager Howard Kendall.

"It is often the case that you can judge where a club is going by who they sign and when Gary McAllister decided to choose them above other top clubs it was clear that they were aiming for a great deal more than First Division survival. It quickly became apparent that they were going to have a real go for the game's biggest prizes.

"Having a man like Howard Wilkinson at the helm was absolutely crucial because, as a high-profile figure with British football, he commands great respect and if you have a solid reputation then you will find that the top players are anxious to come and play for you," he added.

Having signalled their intent by defeating Everton – the 1985 and 1987 League Champions – at Goodison Park on the opening day of the season, Leeds made solid, if unspectacular, progress and by the time they travelled to Merseyside to face Liverpool at Anfield on New Year's Day, 1991, they were up into third place in the table and being talked about as serious Championship contenders. Meeting Liverpool today constitutes the acid test for any side just as it has done for the best part of 25 years and the first League meeting between the two great rivals since the early Eighties was to end in bitter disappointment as the hosts ran out comfortable 3–0 winners. If nothing else that one result showed that while Leeds had taken several giant strides forward since the appointment of Wilkinson, there was still much work to do if fiction was to become fact, if the glory days were to be rediscovered.

Although Leeds remained on the periphery of the race for the title in the remaining four and a half months of the campaign, any hopes of an unexpected success faded once Arsenal had hit their stride in pursuit of a second title in three seasons. Leeds' final placing of fourth, above several allegedly superior sides, vindicated totally Silver's decision to prise his manager away from the clutches of Sheffield Wednesday.

The summer of 1991 brought two more quality signings. Tony Dorigo, the England international left-back, joined from Chelsea for £1.3 million, and £1.6 million – a new club record – was sufficient to tempt Southampton to part with Rod Wallace, one of the quickest forwards in the English game.

Next Steve Hodge was bought from Nottingham Forest at a cost of £900,000 to increase the competition for places in midfield and a further £275,000 was splashed out to tempt Jon Newsome and David Wetherall away from Sheffield Wednesday.

Rather sadly, at a time when Wilkinson was seeking to bolster his squad, he was to lose a key member when Jim Beglin was finally forced to accept that a long-standing knee injury had prematurely ended his career.

The squad was assembled and the scene was set. Privately, Wilkinson and his chairman had set their sights on winning a place in the UEFA Cup. Little did they know that the League Championship, the greatest prize of them all, was just ten months away.

Chapter Three

FROM SMALL ACORNS

While it would be fanciful in the extreme to suggest that any manager could turn round at the end of a season and admit, with any degree of honesty, that his pre-season forecast had proved to be unerringly accurate, Howard Wilkinson would have a stronger case than most were he to suggest that he was an accomplished reader of the crystal ball. Shortly after his Leeds team had defeated Norwich City at Elland Road in the final fixture of a long and demanding campaign, Wilkinson reminded the assembled group of national and provincial sporting journalists of a statement – or perhaps it was a prediction – which he had made back in August, shortly before the opening batch of First Division fixtures. He wasn't boasting or bragging, he was simply reminding those present of the mental target which he had set his players even before a ball had been kicked in anger.

"I said before we started that I felt that any side which managed to get 84 points – or more – and who did not win the League Championship would be unlucky," he said.

"I thought that was a hell of a target for us. I thought that was the absolute ultimate which we could achieve if everything went right for us and if God was good in his heaven. I believed that 84 points would have been an absolutely magnificent achievement for us. We ended up getting 82 points so we very nearly got ten out of ten," he added with a smile.

Wilkinson is something of a rarity amongst modern football managers in so much as he will publicly admit to having set his players both standards and targets to aim for in the weeks and months ahead. Although others are far more reticent to place on record their objectives, Peter Reid, the player-manager of Manchester City, admits that long-term game-plans, be they mental or be they jotted down on paper, are common practice.

"I think that it is fair to say that every manager has a basic idea of what he would like to see his team achieve during the course of a season," he said.

"It is such a predictable thing to do. It probably starts just as soon as the new fixture list is released. Managers will sit down, study the list and say to themselves, 'We should win those two games, draw that one, win those three. . ..' It must happen all the time. It never quite works out as you have planned of course because if every manager in the First Division was accurate in his early assessments, we would have eight or nine clubs tying for the Championship and no one filling the relegation places.

"The fact that you stand to be severely embarrassed if you do get things hopelessly wrong means that most managers keep their feelings, their hopes, very much to themselves. I certainly do. Personally, I can't see the point in boldly stating that my club will do this, or do that because you are on a hiding to nothing. Very, very occasionally, someone will come out of the woodwork and say something totally daft like: 'We are going to win the title.' What usually happens is they finish in mid-table and the national papers have a field day towards the end of the season by reminding everybody of what was said months before," he added.

Wilkinson's target of 84 points constituted an average of two points from every game, or a victory and a draw every two fixtures. It was an exceedingly tall order for a team which, in footballing terms, was still very much wet behind the ears.

After finishing fourth in the previous season, the first appearance in Division One for eight years, expectations were high both at boardroom and terrace level. Those long-suffering supporters who had lived through a bewildering, seemingly endless, period of transition had tasted the forbidden fruit of success, however relative, and found the taste very much to their collective liking.

Rather typically, at a time when United's preparations appeared to be running smoothly things started to go wrong. Tony Dorigo and Mel Sterland were both admitted to hospital for hernia operations, the loss of the former proving to be an acute problem as his absence meant that he was unable to strike up an understanding with his new team-mates during the club's crucial pre-season fixtures.

Amazingly, both men were declared fit and available for the season's opening League fixture against Crystal Palace. Sadly, although the players of both clubs were primed for action, Selhurst Park wasn't. A game which had been eagerly anticipated by everyone connected with Leeds United was postponed because what was described as "essential work" on the ground had not been completed in time. So, as their rivals swung into action in front of predictably large and vociferous opening-day crowds, Wilkinson's players were left kicking not a ball but their heels.

Thankfully, Elland Road was ready and three days later, Nottingham Forest made the short trip up the M1 to fire the opening shots in what was to be a season of glorious entertainment and unexpected triumph. Invariably, the game proved to be fiercely contested and very tight. Forest, who had beaten Leeds, 4–3, on the final day of the previous season, carved out numerous chances but failed to add a cutting edge to some useful and diligent midfield play. Leeds created several inviting openings but converted just one when Gary McAllister swept home from amid a cluster of players. It was enough – just.

Four days after that winning start, Leeds were indebted to the predatory instincts of Steve Hodge who bundled home a very late equaliser to secure a 1–1 draw against Sheffield Wednesday at Elland Road. The true significance of Hodge's dramatic, late strike would not become clear until nine months later when the race for the League Championship entered its final few strides. Had Wednesday secured victory on that warm Saturday afternoon in late August things could have been so very different, such was the manner in which Trevor Francis' side finished the campaign. All goals are important but, in retrospect, Hodge's first for the club was absolutely crucial.

Gary McAllister recalls: "When we assembled at the start of the season it was only natural that we, the players, should discuss amongst ourselves exactly what we thought we were capable of. We had done well in the previous season. By finishing in fourth position we had surprised a lot of people, both supporters and managers of other clubs, and we were obviously very anxious to make even greater strides forward.

"Having had a very close look at the First Division, we knew that finishing high enough up in the table to guarantee a place in Europe was definitely a realistic target. It was within our reach and we were all keen to try and achieve that.

"Before the season started, the manager hadn't told us to aim for anything in particular. He just told us to go out, play to our full abilities and do our best. Having said that, he would set points targets for particular groups of games that were coming up. He would suggest that we were capable of picking up, say, 11 points from the next four League games. It was his way of trying to keep us on our toes.

"Because the manager had brought in Tony Dorigo and Rod Wallace – two very good players – we knew that we had a stronger side than in the previous season. We also knew that people were possibly expecting us to top what we had achieved during that season and win a place in the First Division's top three. It was never going to be easy, we knew that all too well, but we were confident.

"I was feeling good. I had decided to join Leeds because I thought I would have a very good chance of winning things here. Before I had left Leicester City, during talks with the manager and Bill Fotherby, the club's managing director, I had been very impressed by their outlook on life. It quickly became clear to me that they were after much more than just a place in the First Division. They had won promotion but they didn't just want the club to survive in the top bracket, they wanted success. I liked their attitude, which explains why I signed for them.

"That first season was one hell of an experience for me because after playing in front of much smaller, less enthusiastic, crowds at Filbert Street I could hardly believe the support which this club enjoys. Everyone connected with Leeds United is so passionate about their football. The Leeds fans are as good as you will find anywhere in British football – easily on a par with the supporters of Glasgow Rangers, Glasgow Celtic, Liverpool or Manchester United.

"Sometimes fans can make all the difference. When you walk out at Elland Road these days you know it will be full and that the noise will be deafening. We thrive on that sort of atmosphere whereas our opponents can be really put off their game by it. It really is a tremendous help. If anything, our travelling support is even better. It is terrific to walk out on to the pitch of a rival and be greeted by thousands and thousands of screaming Leeds fans. You can almost believe that you are at home sometimes.

"After the disappointment of having our opening game against Crystal Palace postponed, we were really pleased to get off to a winning start against Nottingham Forest. The victory was made all the sweeter from a personal point of view as I managed to get the only goal of the game.

"I actually think we were a little bit fortunate to pick up a point against Sheffield Wednesday because, overall, I would have to say that they outplayed us on the day. They must have felt desperately unhappy about losing two points because we looked out of it until Steve Hodge popped up with a late equaliser. Steve has a habit of scoring really crucial goals. If you look back at the record of our season, he didn't actually score that many but the ones he did get were invariably important.

"Steve's goal did far more than win us a valuable point, it also ensured that we did not surrender an unbeaten home record at a ridiculously early stage. From a mental point of view it is very important to remain unbeaten for as long as you can. Success – an unbeaten sequence – breeds confidence and had we lost to Wednesday we would all have felt terribly downhearted and deflated. Teams who come along to Elland Road to face Leeds United know that they are in for a very tough game. It would have really damaged our confidence if we had lost that game.

"Because we had done so well at home in the previous season we knew, full well, that teams would come to our place and shut up shop in an attempt to keep us out. Although it is always difficult to play against opposition who have decided they will settle for a point it is actually quite flattering because it is a sign of total respect."

Having played one game fewer than their major rivals, Leeds lay in tenth place in Division One when they travelled down to The Dell to face a Southampton side which was quite possibly already preparing for a prolonged fight for survival. Rod Wallace's return to the club where he had established himself as a player of genuine quality could hardly have gone any better and he had a hand in two of the goals as Leeds exposed the glaring deficiencies within the Saints' fragile rearguard to romp home, 4–0, with both Gordon Strachan and Gary Speed hitting the target twice. It was United's first truly inspirational performance of the season – but not the last.

Next stop was Old Trafford, the so-called "theatre of dreams", and the first of four meetings with the team which was to make such a memorable contribution to one of the most fascinating title battles in living memory.

Traditionally, Leeds fare well at Old Trafford but Alex Ferguson's expensively assembled side had started the season well. Indeed, in their opening four League games they had picked up ten points without conceding a solitary goal. However, 406 minutes into a campaign which many armchair experts had foolishly predicted was almost certain to end in Championship glory, the Manchester United defence finally cracked when Lee Chapman, a notoriously slow starter in terms of goals, struck to claim his first of the season.

On a playing surface which, even at that early stage, was proving to be problematical to both sets of players,

Leeds equipped themselves well and as the game entered its final quarter, victory, if not an absolute certainty, did seem highly probable. But for the never-say-die spirit of one Bryan Robson, Leeds would definitely have headed back home to Yorkshire with three points. So many matches of significance were to follow in the months which lay ahead but had Robson not levelled the scores, very late in the game, the whole course of the title battle could well have been changed.

First Division table at the end of August:

1. Manchester United	P 5	W 3	D 2	L 0	Pts 11
2. Liverpool	P 5	W 3	D 1	L 1	Pts 10
6. Leeds United	P 4	W 2	D 2	L 0	Pts 8

Gary McAllister reflects: "I thought that we played tremendously well against Southampton at The Dell. Although they have really struggled in recent years, it is always a difficult ground to go to and to get a satisfactory result because like a lot of sides in the First Division they always have to place such a heavy reliance on their home form. The style in which certain teams play does suit us and Southampton are one of them because even when they are struggling, they always like to try and play open, attractive football – especially in front of their own supporters. The final scoreline of 4–0 might suggest that we dominated the game from the first whistle to the last but that wasn't actually the case because they also had their moments. It was just that we scored at the right times and eventually managed to break their spirit.

"Rod Wallace must have really enjoyed returning to his former club. I know how badly he wanted to score but he played well and had a hand in two of our goals. Whenever you return to one of your old clubs you are always keyed up and anxious to do well. Sometimes you want to show your old club that they were wrong to let you go; sometimes, if it is you who decided that you wanted to leave, you just want to remind them what you are capable of – what they are missing. There is nothing malicious in it, you just want to put on a good display in front of those fans who used to urge you along.

"Winning games away from home is so vital if you are to keep in touch with what is happening at the top of the

Division, so we all left the south coast in a very happy frame of mind. It used to be the case that if a side could win its home games and draw away from home there was a fairly reasonable chance of success come the end of May. It has changed. These days you need to win quite a few matches on your travels. Avoiding defeat away from home is, quite simply, no longer enough. The introduction of the three points for a win system was certainly instrumental in changing attitudes.

"I remember the game against Manchester United at Old Trafford particularly well. Playing there is always a memorable event because it is such an imposing stadium for a player to perform in. On top of that, the ground always seems to be full.

"When we played there this season, it was unbelievably hot out on the pitch; it must have been about 95 degrees and unless you are a very special athlete, the heat does take its toll. Anyway, it was boiling out there which quite possibly explains why the match wasn't quite the classic encounter it could have been.

"Apart from realising that Manchester United would be one of our main rivals, that afternoon proved to me that Bryan Robson was still one hell of a good player. He was one of the few people out there who was able to completely ignore the baking heat and carry on in his normal, assured way. He ran up and down that pitch like a whippet, chasing every loose ball and contesting every tackle. He played superbly for 90 minutes and it didn't surprise me in the least that it was he who popped up near the end to scramble home United's equalising goal.

"It is strange, you know, people have been writing off Robson for a couple of years now but he still delivers the goods whenever he plays. He is a player I have admired for many, many years and although it has been suggested that he is now ready to pack up playing – certainly at the top level – and move forward into management, I suspect he will still be pulling on the red shirt next season in one last attempt to win the Championship medal which has so far eluded him.

"Very few teams would leave Old Trafford complaining about only having secured a draw but we felt slightly annoyed with ourselves simply because we were within sight of the final whistle when United finally managed to get their goal. Even so, it was a case of one point won rather than two points lost. I suppose that if you can travel to the ground of one of your main rivals and get a commendable draw then you have to be happy in the final count.

"By the end of August we found ourselves sitting in sixth place which wasn't bad at all bearing in mind that most, if not all, of the teams above us in the table had played one game more. We were undefeated, playing well and still very much in touch."

While it is possibly true to say that, early in a season, no one game is any more important than the rest, Leeds' next game was crucial, not so much in terms of accruing valuable points but in terms of appraising the character development of a side which was still relatively inexperienced. The visit of the defending champions, Arsenal, to Elland Road proved to be something of a watershed in Leeds' season in many respects because it showed exactly what Wilkinson's side was capable of when faced by mounting adversity.

In the absence of Chris Fairclough, who had suffered a serious knee injury against Southampton which was to keep him on the sidelines for five, frustrating weeks, Wilkinson again selected John McClelland, a bold and brave move bearing in mind the speed and mobility of the Arsenal forward line.

For long periods, Arsenal played like true champions and few of those present would have disputed their right to a two-goal lead, one which gave every indication of deciding the outcome. However, at the very point when they appeared to be down and out – at the precise moment all seemed lost – Leeds rallied. Goals by Gordon Strachan and Lee Chapman restored the status quo and as a fascinating game neared its climax Arsenal, after dominating for so long, were left hanging on as they grimly fought to avoid defeat. As the national press was to emphasise the following day, Leeds, to a man, had displayed the fighting spirit which their manager had demanded before the start of the season.

28

Gary McAllister says: "It doesn't really matter what sort of form Arsenal are in when you play them because they are one of the most accomplished teams in the English game without any doubt.

"We knew, very well, that we were going to be in for a very tough afternoon and we were not to be disappointed. I was really impressed by them. They played some lovely, one-touch stuff against us and, I must admit, when they scored their second goal, I thought we were out of it. But one of the good things about this Leeds team is that we just don't give up. It might be a cliché to say that a football match lasts for 90 minutes but, nonetheless, it is true. You have to keep going right to the end even when things don't look too good for you. One of the features of our season was our ability to grind out good results when we were not playing very well. That is something which you have to do. No team can play well all the time so it is important that you pick up points during these difficult patches. We didn't perform particularly well against Arsenal but our spirit and our determination carried us through and brought us a valuable point."

By the time Manchester City arrived at Elland Road on 7 September it had become clear that Manchester intended to launch a two-pronged assault on the Championship. Having recovered from the shock of losing manager Howard Kendall, City had begun to flourish under the astute leadership of Peter Reid, a man who personifies northern grit and who was successfully waging a war against advancing years. City were going well and in Niall Quinn and David White they possessed one of the most formidable and productive strike-forces in the First Division.

At the conclusion of a game which was played at a predictably frenetic pace, Leeds ran out 3–0 winners with goals by Tony Dorigo, Gordon Strachan and – amazingly – David Batty. Batty's goal, a marvellous solo effort which embraced close control and a superb sense of balance, was only the second of his career and, ridiculous though it may seem, the very first at Elland Road in front of supporters who had long admired his midfield artistry but bemoaned his wayward shooting. His only other goal had been scored 160 games and 45 months earlier.

Batty admitted at the time: "Other people seem to have been more concerned than I have that I had not scored for so long. I know that scoring is a side of my game that needs to be improved if I am to become a complete player."

When the season was over, and when Howard Wilkinson was called upon to select his team's most important and outstanding performances, he did not hesitate to single out the victory over City. "At the time, they were going like a train so we did well to win 3–0," he said with typical modesty.

The defeat of City lifted Leeds up into fourth place in the table, a position which was to be improved upon seven days later when Carl Shutt scored the only goal of the game to put paid to Chelsea at Stamford Bridge. Shutt, a more than competent striker who was to spend most of the season filling in for injured team-mates, had been drafted into the senior side as a replacement for Rod Wallace, who had damaged a knee against City. He was not to return to action until late October on the day Leeds finally moved to the top of the table.

When Leeds travelled down to Coventry City's Highfield Road, they were up into second place – they were never to drop out of the top two for the remainder of the season. But for once Leeds' normally prolific and reliable forwards were found to be firing blanks and although Coventry enjoyed some moments of genuine good fortune, they held on for a draw.

Leeds were to create a small, but certainly not insignificant, piece of history in their next fixture when the old enemy from the Sixties and Seventies, Liverpool, crossed the Pennines.

Leeds had not actually managed to beat the Merseysiders in 18 long years. The last time the white of Yorkshire had triumphed over the red of Lancashire had been back in the 1973-74 season when a Mick Jones goal had given Leeds the slenderest of wins at Elland Road. In 1991, the margin was exactly the same with Steve Hodge the unlikely goal-scoring hero in what was his first full appearance for his new club. Things tend to run full-circle in sport, as in life, and just as the team of 1973 went on to lift the title, so too did the team of 1991.

Gary McAllister comments: "We were all fully aware that Leeds hadn't beaten Liverpool for years and years and while that didn't actually enter into our thinking as we prepared for the game, I suppose it did give us that extra little incentive to go out and do the business.

"Games against Liverpool are always high-profile. That is something which is unavoidable simply because of their pedigree and because of the enormously high standards which they have set over the past 25 years. Their record really is phenomenal and they are still very much the yardstick by which all other clubs must judge themselves. When a team does beat Liverpool, whether it is at home or at Anfield, the news travels far and wide very quickly indeed. They have been so consistent that every one of their defeats is greeted with surprise.

"That victory was vital for us in more ways than one because it meant that people really did have to start taking us seriously – if they hadn't been doing that already. I am certain that the scoreline, Leeds United 1 Liverpool 0, made people all over the country sit up and take notice.

"Perhaps those who had previously been regarding us as something of a flash in the pan began to realise that we *were* a good team and that we were not going to slip away quietly and let the more fashionable clubs get on with fighting over the League title.

"I think that it is fair to say that we possibly started the season as most people's fourth favourites to win the Championship. I would imagine that most people would have placed Liverpool, Arsenal and Manchester United ahead of us. After we had defeated Liverpool – still a very strong side despite their injury problems – perhaps people began to consider us as real contenders.

"That result extended our unbeaten sequence to nine games which was a tremendous way to start the season. Although we were up near the top and a few people – not very many, I hasten to add – had been bold enough to suggest that we did look capable of staying there, the manager still went out of his way to try and ensure that we did not come under any pressure.

"He never once sat down and talked about us possibly becoming the champions of English football. That just isn't his style at all. He just kept telling us to carry on the good work and to concentrate on what we had discussed and what we had gone through out on the training ground. His approach to things – a very laid-back approach – certainly helped a great deal.

"What also helped us was the fact that everyone – newspapers, ex-professionals, other managers – was telling Manchester United that it was they who were the favourites. Arsenal's form was patchy, Liverpool were struggling with a series of injuries to key players like Ian Rush, John Barnes and Ronnie Whelan, so it was almost assumed that Manchester United would take the title race by the throat. Being regarded as outsiders did help us a lot."

Chapter Four

CONSOLIDATE AND PROSPER

Having not only kept pace with the early-season front-runners but also consolidated their place in the First Division's top two, Leeds were faced by the intimidating prospect of four away games in their next batch of six League fixtures. However, having produced performances of character and great style at Southampton and Chelsea, travelling away from Elland Road was something to relish and savour. The word, fear, was one which was swiftly being eradicated from the players' vocabulary.

Rather like Southampton, Norwich City have acquired the uncanny knack of winning a very high percentage of their games at home in recent seasons and they had earned a reputation for overturning the proverbial form-book and delivering shock results. Leeds fared better than most, although it is debatable whether or not a 2–2 draw was regarded as a success or as a failure bearing in mind that Manchester United defeated Tottenham Hotspur at White Hart Lane on the same afternoon.

Top of the First Division at the end of September:

1. Manchester United   P 10   W 8   D 2   L 0   Pts 26
2. Leeds United   P 10   W 5   D 5   L 0   Pts 20

The first day of October was a date which no one at the club will care to remember as it signalled Leeds' first defeat of the season in what was their twelfth competitive, senior fixture. Six weeks after being declared unfit for professional football, Selhurst Park was ready for Leeds United. Sadly, so too were Crystal Palace.

Since taking over at Elland Road in the winter of 1988, Howard Wilkinson has continually won praise for the gracious manner in which he accepts defeat. It is to his eternal credit that whatever the outcome, he is always more than willing to meet the media after matches to discuss, in a frank, usually amusing, manner what has transpired during the course of the previous 90 minutes. Few managers in the First Division are more approachable, few are more direct – none are quite so honest.

To say that Wilkinson was upset by the 1–0 defeat at Selhurst Park would be something of an understatement. It wasn't so much the loss of the three points on offer which left him feeling somewhat dazed and perplexed but the manner of a defeat which few had been anticipating. An evenly contested game had provided both sides with several opportunities to break the deadlock but poor finishing and some excellent goalkeeping had ensured that the stalemate was to prevail. As the game neared its climax, and as both sides began to tire, a goalless draw seemed assured.

Although the evening had been relatively free of incident and neither trainer had been called upon to treat any serious injuries, the match, much to the amazement of those present, was allowed to go on . . . and on . . . and on. It appeared that the referee had decided that he was going to play until someone – anyone – scored a decisive goal. Palace duly obliged when they profited from the highly dubious award of a free kick, just outside the penalty area.

At a conservative estimate, the goal which finally ended Leeds' splendid unbeaten record came in the 94th minute although several, normally reliable, journalists who were in attendance on that night would swear that it was scored as late as the 96th or 97th minute.

Gary McAllister recalls: "Obviously we were bitterly disappointed to lose a match for the first time all season. What made it even worse was the timing of Palace's winning goal because it seemed to come so very late on.

"I had to come off near the end of the game after a collision with Geoff Thomas and from where I was, the

34

last five minutes seemed endless. I'm not sure exactly when they scored but it was deep – very, very deep – into added time. I don't even think they should have been awarded the free-kick from which they scored but in this game you have to take the rough with the smooth. Sometimes the breaks go for you, sometimes they go against you and they definitely went against us that night.

"It was a game which we should never have lost because I thought that we were clearly the better team throughout. If you are outplayed by someone and you lose then fair enough; that is something which, while disappointing, you have to accept. But, if you play well and lose, that is a totally different thing. Obviously, I am slightly biased but we deserved to leave London with at least a point. With a little more luck we could have even won the game.

"We don't like losing at this club but it was vitally important that we forget all about the Palace game and look to the immediate future. Even if you have lost in controversial circumstances there is absolutely no point at all in dwelling on things because, as they say, what is done is done. We tried to be positive straight afterwards; we didn't think of what might have been, we concentrated on our next game."

That next game was, to say the very least, a bizarre affair. Sheffield United, forceful, belligerent but woefully inconsistent, were struggling near the foot of the table after another disastrous opening to the season. On paper at least, it was the mismatch of the day – aristocrats against alley-cats. Someone once said that football was a funny game and this match seemed to have been designed to lend credence to that particular adage.

Leeds began as if the Championship itself rested on the outcome. After having scored just four times in their previous five League games the floodgates opened and Dave Bassett's side was taken apart at the very seams. Mel Sterland and Steve Hodge both struck twice as the prospect of an embarrassing demolition began to loom large on the horizon. Perhaps sensing that far sterner tasks lay ahead in the coming weeks, Leeds inexplicably removed their foot from the accelerator. Sheffield United had almost been invited to punish an uncharacteristic bout of generosity and, not too surprisingly, they were more than happy to oblige.

In one of the most astonishing fight-backs of the season, the men from Bramall Lane threatened to turn logic on its head. Goals by Hoyland, Agana and Bradshaw undermined Leeds' confidence to such an extent that the final whistle could not come soon enough.

Gary McAllister recalls his feelings: "It is strange to feel a great sense of relief after leading by four clear goals but these strange things do sometimes happen in football. Although I must compliment Sheffield United for the way they played that day in so much as they never gave up trying even when everything did appear to be lost, I do believe there were mitigating circumstances.

"I had to come off injured as did Mel Sterland and that changed the whole rhythm of our game and the whole shape of the match itself. Our final margin of victory may have been very narrow but I do feel that we deserved to win because before Sheffield United launched that dramatic late come-back, we played some really fine football and looked likely to score every time we went into their half of the field."

Chris Fairclough was ready to return for the next game against Notts County at Meadow Lane after missing a total of nine games. Another man just happy to pull on a white shirt was Chris Kamara who was named as a substitute after an absence of 11 months because of an ankle problem.

For the second game in a row, Leeds proved to be in menacing mood, again finding the rear of the opposition's net on four occasions, Hodge claiming the 100th goal of his career to add to strikes by Chris Whyte, Lee Chapman and Gary McAllister. County, whose First Division future was already in some doubt and the subject of much local debate, did manage to score twice but it was nothing more than a token gesture.

Gary McAllister and the other Leeds lads were well pleased: "Now that was a really good performance by us. It was just one of those days when our football flowed

36

without a great deal of effort. You sometimes get afternoons when you are really in the mood and that was one of them.

"I don't score quite as many goals as I possibly should but I did get one that day. It was a long-range drive. I just fancied my chances – as we all did."

In many respects the 1–0 victory over Oldham Athletic at Elland Road on the following Saturday was slightly fortuitous, earned as it was by a Brian Kilcline own goal, but, again, it constituted history in the making. On the same afternoon, just 35 miles down the M1, Manchester United's unbeaten League record was being ended at Hillsborough by Sheffield Wednesday. Kilcline obviously did not know it at the time but by pushing the ball beyond his own goalkeeper he had guaranteed that Leeds would move to the top of the First Division table for the first time since they last won the title back in 1974.

Top of the First Division at the end of October:

1. Leeds United	P 14	W 8	D 5	L 1	Pts 29
2. Manchester United	P 13	W 8	D 4	L 1	Pts 28

The joy felt by Wilkinson and his players was, however, to be short-lived. The following weekend Leeds were unable to find a way through an unyielding Wimbledon defence at Plough Lane during the course of a dour goalless draw while Manchester United defeated Sheffield United, 2–0, at Old Trafford. The pattern of uncertainty and unpredictability had been set and the leadership of the First Division was to change several more times before the season inched towards its dramatic finale.

Gary McAllister assesses the situation: "Beating Oldham Athletic was very important to us because everyone kept telling me that they were Leeds' bogey team and that they always did well against us, irrespective of whether the game was being played at Elland Road or Boundary Park.

"They are a very difficult side to play against because they are quite solid at the back and they have the ability to break forward quickly. Joe Royle did well to sign Graeme Sharp from Everton during the summer because he is always a handful up front.

"I suppose you could say that we were a little fortunate to beat them as the game's only goal was an own goal but luck does tend to even itself out during the course of a long season. We played reasonably well on the day but we were all aware that we could do much better. We were also all aware that we would have to do much better if we were going to keep ourselves up near the top and sustain our challenge for the title.

"Obviously, we had no idea at all what was happening to Manchester United on that day but it was a pleasant surprise to get back into the dressing-room and hear that they had lost out at Sheffield Wednesday. It was a little strange to sit down and look at the First Division table and see the name of Leeds United perched at the very top. Just 14 months after winning promotion from the Second Division, the club was back on top of English football.

"It was a terrific feeling to be at the top. Although we had started a little sluggishly, we had played some attractive and entertaining football along the way. Even then, we never really talked about the possibility of us winning the big prize. I knew that it was starting to look pretty good for us but there was still such a long way to go. It would have been extremely foolish of us if we had started to believe our own good publicity.

"We were happy and content with the way things were shaping up for us but, as anyone involved with professional football will tell you, you can't win the Championship in October. Consistency is the name of the game and that is what we were aiming for."

November is traditionally the month when the First Division finally begins to take some sort of shape. With one third of the season gone, it is usually clear to all but the most blinkered exactly who will be contesting the Championship and who will be fighting to preserve their current status.

Apart from the disappointing draw against Wimbledon, it was a tremendous month for Leeds and the leadership of the Division was reclaimed on the 16th when Queen's Park Rangers proferred only limited resistance en route to a 2–0 defeat. The game marked the beginning of what could be described as Rod Wallace's purple patch for he scored his first-ever League goal for his new club and subsequently grew in confidence and stature to such an extent that he was to find the target in each of the next four fixtures. The other man on target on an afternoon when Leeds proved conclusively that they were more than capable of "rolling over" indifferent opposition was Mel Sterland. It was the 50th League goal of his career.

The glare of publicity beckoned the following Sunday afternoon when Leeds' growing stature was underlined by their appearance on live television. It was wholly predictable that the broadcasting moguls would select the game against Aston Villa at Villa Park for live transmission, for under Ron Atkinson the Birmingham club was, at last, threatening to make its mark in Division One. Had Wilkinson and his team not approached the game in the right frame of mind there is no question that negotiating the afternoon with any comfort would have been extremely difficult. Villa, reliable at the back and pacey up front, had proved themselves to be capable of beating anyone on their day. This was not to be their day. This was Leeds' day.

In front of an armchair audience which ran into millions, Wilkinson's buoyant team gave a stark reminder of both its quality and its intent. Not to put too fine a point on things, Villa were ruthlessly dismantled in a manner which left Atkinson and his right-hand man, Andy Gray, shaking their heads in absolute disbelief. Sterland, Wallace and Chapman, with two, got the goals in an emphatic 4–1 win but, in truth, Leeds enjoyed such overwhelming superiority in every department that the final margin of victory should have been cavernous and not simply huge.

Chapman's brace – the second of which was a superb diving header – took his tally to 51 goals in just 96 games since he joined the club from Nottingham Forest in January 1990. Not at all bad for a much-maligned forward who was to prove his literary worth shortly afterwards by penning a series of compelling features for *The Times*.

Gary McAllister comments: "I think we proved during the course of the season that television and the live broadcasting of our games seemed to turn us on. I don't know whether it was coincidental or not but on almost every occasion we were featured on television, we played exceptionally well.

"I think those people whose job it is to plan future broadcasts must have fallen in love with us because whenever they selected us we seemed to come up with the goods by banging in plenty of goals. It was good for their ratings and it was good for our morale and for our League position.

"There is a psychological aspect to performing well in front of the cameras because it goes without saying that most professional footballers like nothing better than to sit down on a Sunday afternoon and watch a live game. Now, if you are scheduled to meet someone in the next couple of weeks and they see what you are capable of, I think, perhaps, it can help you. It certainly can't do you any harm, can it?

"It goes without saying that we played well against Aston Villa. In fact, although we turned in quite a few very, very useful displays during the season, I, personally, think it was our best of the lot. Just as we had done by defeating Liverpool at Elland Road in September, I think we proved our worth on that day. I think we again underlined our growing confidence and, hopefully, we also managed to scare a few people.

"It was after that game that some of the newspapers began to change their attitude towards us; they suddenly started to suggest that we might just have the all-round ability to stay in the hunt for the title. There is nothing better than playing well, winning convincingly and then picking up the papers the next day to see what the reaction has been.

"Everything went right for us at Villa Park. Chris Fairclough was asked to do a man-to-man job on their danger man, Tony Daley, and he marked him out of the game completely. Mel Sterland pushed forward into the right-hand side of midfield and Lee Chapman was his usual reliable self up front. Yes, it was a wonderful day for all of us."

40

After a bright start to the season which had included a magnificent win over Arsenal and an encouraging draw against Manchester United, Everton had begun to falter badly and despite the injection of new talent, they were stranded in mid-table by the time they arrived at Elland Road on 30 November.

The Merseysiders' manager, Howard Kendall, had long insisted that his team was actually a good deal better than was suggested by their League placing and he had promised Leeds an uncomfortable afternoon. He obviously wasn't joking. By utilising to its fullest effect the brilliance of Peter Beardsley and the trickery of Peter Beagrie, Everton did, indeed, provide very stiff opposition, and had their finishing matched their smooth and inventive approach play it is conceivable that the visitors could have won a fiercely competitive match with something to spare.

As the game edged towards the final whistle, Everton appeared to have done enough to claim a point. Fortunately, they were not the first side to underestimate Leeds' grim determination. Time was running out when Rod Wallace crashed a volley beyond Neville Southall to decide the issue.

Sadly, the afternoon was not without incident, Chris Fairclough being sent off after an unsavoury, if seemingly innocuous, clash with Mark Ward. Both Fairclough and Howard Wilkinson disputed the legality of the decision but a plea to allow the centre-back to use video evidence as a means of defence was denied by the game's unsympathetic hierarchy. "The player can understandably feel that justice has not been done," said Wilkinson as if to prove himself the master of the understatement.

Gary McAllister agrees: "This was another of those games where we were required to sit tight, keep our formation and grind out a result. We didn't play particularly well but, to be fair, Everton pushed us all the way and they too had their fair share of good chances.

"It was disappointing to see Chris Fairclough sent off but the less said about that the better. It was pleasing to be able to win a game with only ten men out on the field at the final whistle."

Top of the First Division at the end of November:

1. Leeds United	P 18	W 11	D 6	L 1	Pts 39
2. Manchester United	P 17	W 11	D 5	L 1	Pts 38

With the festive season just around the corner, David Batty presented the Leeds supporters with an early Christmas box when he put the finishing touches to a new, four-year contract. Batty's decision to pledge his long-term future to his home-town club was to finally put an end to prolonged speculation that he was, in some way, unsettled at Elland Road and that rumours of a move to another leading First Division club – quite possibly Liverpool – were totally inaccurate.

Having tried, but failed, to establish himself as a first-team regular at Leeds, Chris Kamara finally bowed to the inevitable in late November and joined Luton Town in a £150,000 transfer. His uncompromising approach to mid-field play had endeared him to the fans on the terraces and he was afforded a hero's welcome when he returned with his new club in late February.

The Leeds success story now began to gather fresh momentum and Howard Wilkinson was named as the Barclay's Manager of the Month for October while Gary Speed was the choice as the Barclay's Young Eagle for the same period.

December was to prove a largely disappointing month as the first signs of battle fatigue began to surface. Although goals by Rod Wallace and Speed were sufficient to dispose of Kamara's new club at Kenilworth Road, the impetus was lost thereafter and the next four League games ended in draws so allowing Manchester United to return to the summit of the First Division for the first time in more than six weeks.

An entertaining game against the thoroughbreds of Tottenham Hotspur at Elland Road ended in a 1–1 draw and there were no goals the following weekend when Leeds visited the City Ground to face a Nottingham Forest side which had already abandoned all hope of making any impression in the Championship race.

Boxing Day brought struggling Southampton to Elland Road but an uncharacteristically poor defensive display was instrumental in allowing two precious points to slip away. Leading 3–1, courtesy of two goals by Steve Hodge and one by Gary Speed, Leeds seemed assured of victory until Southampton staged an improbable late rally to score twice in the dying minutes.

It was somewhat fitting that Leeds' final fixture of a year which brought so much success should be against Manchester United – time-honoured rivals from across the Pennines and closest, perhaps only, contenders for the Championship. Inevitably, Elland Road was bursting at the seams as the First Division's two heavyweights thundered into each other in front of the television cameras. Victory for Leeds would have returned them to the top of the table; victory for Manchester United would have pushed them five points clear at the top and, with two crucial games in hand, it would have served to underline their position as the clear favourites.

It was a tough, gruelling game which was often stripped bare of all niceties – it had to be because there was so much at stake. One slip by either side and the destiny of the title could have been irreversibly altered. Few were surprised when the game ended as a draw, Neil Webb opening the scoring for the visitors only for Mel Sterland to confidently fire home a late penalty after Gary McAllister had been bundled to the ground by Gary Pallister.

Top of the First Division at the end of December:

1. Manchester United	P 21	W 14	D 6	L 1	Pts 48
2. Leeds United	P 23	W 12	D 10	L 1	Pts 46
3. Sheffield Wednesday	P 22	W 11	D 6	L 5	Pts 39
4. Manchester City	P 23	W 11	D 6	L 6	Pts 39
5. Aston Villa	P 22	W 11	D 3	L 8	Pts 36

Gary McAllister reflects on that period: "December always tends to be a tricky sort of a month because the games seem to come thick and fast. Although we were disappointed to drop two points against Tottenham, it was a game which I enjoyed playing in very much indeed. Tottenham are the sort of side who will always try and play football even if they are having a bad time. It was a very open game which could have gone either way. In the end, I think a draw was probably a fair result.

"The game at the City Ground was another good one because, again, both teams went out to play good, open football. It was to end goalless but that just goes to prove that, sometimes, games do not necessarily require goals to entertain the paying public.

"The Southampton game was one that really stuck in our throats for weeks afterwards. Normally, we can forget poor performances very quickly at this club but that really annoyed all the players because we threw the game away. We were coasting along quite happily with a comfortable two-goal advantage and then we let it slip by giving away two very bad goals.

"After that sort of thing has happened to a team they just can't wait to get out on to the pitch and put things right. After that major disappointment, the next game couldn't come quickly enough.

"There is an old saying in football which suggests that if a team is still involved at Christmas – still in contention – then they have got a real chance. Although we had carelessly thrown away two points against Southampton we were still in second place, just behind Manchester United.

"We were happy enough with that. I think that if someone had said, at the start of the season, that we would be in that sort of position at Christmas we would have settled for it. The important thing was that we had shown people that we could play and we had proved that we could sustain a real challenge. We had overcome disappointments and injuries to key players and we were still in there with a great chance of winning the title."

Like McAllister, Everton manager Howard Kendall firmly believes that the congested Christmas and New Year period is of paramount importance to any side with designs on the League Championship.

"I have always regarded that part of the season as arguably the most important of the entire campaign. If a team can enter January in good form, the psychological effect can be both immense and decisive. It is almost as if players, having passed the half-way stage, can visualise the finishing post in the distance. They can see exactly where it is they are going and if they are still in with a shout, they collectively gird their loins and redouble their effort," he said.

"Having managed to reach Christmas with only one defeat in the League it was pretty obvious that Leeds had a chance. I still wasn't completely convinced that they would have the stamina to go all the way but they had impressed everyone with their fine football and their ultra-competitive edge.

"I know that very many people had already suggested that the Championship had been reduced to the proverbial two-horse race but I couldn't subscribe to that point of view. It was a ludicrous thing to say because with so many games left to play there was still so much that could happen. Liverpool were beginning to grow steadily stronger as their injury problems began to clear up, my old club, Manchester City, were still going along quite nicely and you still couldn't rule out Arsenal because they are one of the few sides capable of stringing together seven or eight straight wins.

"It wasn't over by a very long way but Leeds had done exceptionally well to stay in the top two and I felt that the longer they could stay there, the more their confidence would grow. I am sure that Howard Wilkinson will have been a very happy man as he sat down for his lunch on Christmas Day.

"Although Howard had deliberately attempted to keep the pressure off his players by refusing to even discuss the likely outcome of the Championship, I suspect he will have taken a sly look at his side's remaining programme around this time to see what was coming up in the weeks ahead," he added.

Chapter Five

WHAT MIGHT HAVE BEEN: THE PROFESSIONAL VIEW

But for a display of loyalty which was both typical and understandable, it is conceivable that the task of steering Leeds United forward into a new era would have been handed not to Howard Wilkinson – but to Howard Kendall.

In October of 1988 – a winter of discontent if ever there was one – Billy Bremner was summoned to Elland Road and dismissed, his dream of restoring the club to a position of prominence within English football over. With one brief, albeit predictable, action the Leeds hierarchy had officially brought down the curtain on the Revie era.

Bremner, the third member of the famous side of the Seventies to fail in his attempts to stoke up the dying embers of a dwindling fire, was gone; the natural line of progression from dressing-room to managerial office was finally at an end and the search was on to secure the services of an "outsider", someone of proven ability with the courage to brandish a new broom to sweep clean a club which was sustained only by the fast-fading memories of past glories.

Inevitably, the media, both local and national, were swift to provide an uneasy, anxious support with a lengthy list of possible contenders. After a series of top-level meetings, the Leeds board isolated Kendall as the man who was best suited to the job.

In many respects Kendall was not only the logical choice, but the only choice. After initially struggling to transform the fortunes of Everton, the club which he had served with such distinction as a player, Kendall had struck gold during the mid-Eighties. In four glorious seasons he had used his considerable business acumen and natural flair to lead the Merseyside club to two League Championships, the FA Cup and the European Cup Winners Cup. He was being courted as a possible manager of the England national side and he was, arguably, the most sought after manager in European football.

There was, however, a problem. After Everton's title success in 1987, Kendall had severed his ties with English football and headed for Spain. As coach of the leading Basque club, Athletico Bilbao, he was successful, content and settled. Luring him back to a Second Division club of debatable quality and largely unknown potential was going to be difficult. Undeterred by the fact that Newcastle United had already failed in a bid to tempt Kendall back to his native north-east, Leeds studiously set about landing their man.

Kendall admits that he was very flattered by Leeds' approach and although he ultimately decided to remain with Bilbao there may well have been a different outcome but for the timing of Leeds' hugely attractive offer. "I was greatly honoured by the interest of both Newcastle United and Leeds United. They are both big and famous clubs and it was really good to know that, while I had moved away to Spain, I had not been forgotten by the people back home," he says.

"To be honest, when I think about it now, I wasn't really tempted by either offer simply because, from my point of view, the timing was all wrong. I had only been at Athletico Bilbao for about 18 months and they had shown such warmth and such loyalty that I simply couldn't walk out. When Leeds did come in for me it was a virtual re-run of what had happened a few weeks earlier when Newcastle came in.

"Like Newcastle, they found themselves without a manager and like Newcastle, they were anxious to find a replacement as quickly as was possible; someone who had a good track record within the English game. Throughout my career, I have always made it perfectly clear that I will *not* enter into negotiations with any English club which still has a man in control. If there is a vacancy – and there was in this case – then that is a totally different matter altogether.

"I have never believed that there is anything wrong with talking to anyone so when Leeds contacted me and asked if I would meet up with them to discuss the situation at Elland Road, I said that I would. Bill Fotherby, the club's managing director, was the man I met and I have to say that he is one of the most persuasive men I have ever met in my life.

"Although I had already decided that I was going to remain in Spain, Bill sold Leeds United to me in a way no one else could have done during the course of the meeting. Believe me, he did everything possible to try and convince me that I should immediately pack my bags and return home . . . well . . . return to West Yorkshire, actually.

"Even though I knew that I would eventually announce that I was going to remain where I was, I went so far as to listen to the terms of the contract which United were willing to offer me. It was intriguing to say the very least. Now, unless I am mistaken, and I don't think I am, the main stipulation was that I had to guarantee that Leeds United would definitely win promotion from the Second Division at the end of my first, full season in charge. Managers can guarantee many, many things but they can never guarantee promotion, irrespective of who they are and what they may have achieved in the past.

"It wasn't made clear to me what would happen to my contract if I failed to end the club's lengthy exile from the First Division – you will have to draw your own conclusions.

"Having turned Leeds down, I was absolutely delighted when they found the man they were looking for in the shape of Howard Wilkinson. In my autobiography, which was published last year, I said that I thought Leeds would go places under Howard Wilkinson and I have been proved right."

Kendall, who is now back at Goodison Park after a brief and controversial spell with Manchester City, is far from surprised at the success which Leeds have achieved under Wilkinson's astute managership and he readily applauds the manner in which he has subtly altered the long-ball game which he employed at his two previous clubs, Notts County and Sheffield Wednesday.

"The simple fact of the matter is that no club has ever won the biggest prize in English football – the League title – by using the long-ball, route-one system; I doubt they ever will.

"Towards the end of his time at Hillsborough, Howard began to change his tactical approach to the game. What had been a very direct system began to have a far more cultured look about it. The reason for this was quite possibly that he began to appreciate that only by altering the style of his team could he hope to make even greater strides forward.

"By marrying two quite differing styles together he did begin to make progress at Wednesday. Exactly how far he would have taken that club, we will, of course, never now know because before he had the time to complete the job, he was on his way to Leeds.

"Howard had obviously learned a great deal from this brief period of experimentation because as soon as he took control at Elland Road he put into practice this idea of using the two techniques. He blended together the long-ball and the more patient, more stylish aspects of what could be termed "real" football. It worked too because, after ensuring that Leeds' Second Division status was to be preserved, he took them to promotion in the following season. They went up as deserved champions and, importantly, with some style.

"Howard is fortunate to have a player like Lee Chapman in his side because he is so adept in the air and so experienced that it gives him so many different options. It means that if the flowing football dries up, or if they are running through an unproductive spell, they can always revert to the good old-fashioned long ball up the centre of the park. If those sort of passes are delivered properly, and often enough, you can bet your life that Chapman will find his way on to the end of most of them.

"After enjoying a tremendous first season back in the top flight when they surpassed everyone's expectations by finishing in fourth place, Howard very wisely went out and strengthened his senior squad. They had made wonderful progress but I think he knew that he required at least three new faces if the momentum was to be maintained and if his side was to launch a realistic challenge for the League Championship.

"After being given the money he wanted, Howard spent it well – he really did. He brought in Rodney Wallace to add pace and flair up front and Steve Hodge to add guile and goalscoring ability in midfield. For me, the best signing of the lot was Tony Dorigo who is a very, very classy footballer, one who contributes as much to attacks as he does to defence. In the final count, the signing of Dorigo may just have made all the difference to Leeds. He could be the difference between winning the League title and finishing, say, as runners-up.

"Actually, the Leeds defence as a whole is very under-rated because the central partnership of Chris Whyte and Chris Fairclough really is excellent. It is quite ironic that those two lads have done so well because, without wishing to sound disrespectful in any way at all, they could be termed as cast-offs. Whyte had been at Arsenal, Crystal Palace and West Bromwich Albion without too much success and Fairclough had failed to establish himself at Nottingham Forest and Tottenham Hotspur. Bringing the two of them together – two men who had a lot to prove – was a very intelligent piece of forward planning.

"Much has been made of Howard's uncanny knack of successfully modifying his tactical approach to suit different occasions and I would be the first to applaud him for that. He has proved himself to be a very sound tactician and during the course of this season whatever he tried seemed to reap a very rich reward. If a manager can change his approach, and if it comes off for him, then his players are much more likely to accept it the next time. If things go well with a new system which the players were possibly initially a little wary of, they will fully embrace it on the next occasion. It does, of course, work both ways because if it goes wrong the lads in the dressing-room will find themselves tempted to fall back on the 'if it isn't broken then don't fix it' theory, which is perfectly understandable. There is a great deal of psychology involved in running a football team in this day and age and I think Howard understands the psyche of the modern player better than most. Again, he deserves full credit for that."

Although Kendall's respect for Wilkinson runs deep, he confesses to being slightly surprised at the speed of the Leeds revolution. "I think Howard fully appreciated he would need new talent if he was to have a real crack at winning the title so he strengthened his defence, his midfield and his attack with the basic aim of keeping it tight at the back and scoring more goals. It has worked.

"Once the pattern of the season was clearly established, it became clear, pretty quickly, that the title was likely to end up either at Old Trafford or at Elland Road. They were both performing with such consistency that those other clubs who started the campaign with designs on the Championship – ourselves, Liverpool, Arsenal, Manchester City and Sheffield Wednesday – were struggling to stay in touch at the top.

"Once they had broken away from the pack it became the proverbial two-horse race until very late in the day when Wednesday and Arsenal began to creep up on the rails. In most people's minds, Manchester United were the firm favourites, which was totally understandable bearing in mind the size of their squad and the size of the Leeds squad. It might be a cliché but it is true to say that the Championship *is* a marathon and you will usually find that the club which can boast the biggest, best and fittest squad will win the day.

"Now, I don't want to sound clever after the event but I always felt that Manchester United were placing too high a reliance upon out-and-out flair to win games. It just seemed to me that they were waiting for someone like Ryan Giggs or Andrei Kanchelskis to produce the one moment of inspirational magic which would prove to be the difference between winning and drawing; the difference between one point and three. Either that or they were looking to Mark Hughes to come up with one of his famous spectacular strikes.

"Basically, I saw them as a flair team who were too often reliant upon individualism whereas Leeds, in stark contrast, were a real team; a well-disciplined and organised unit. Don't get me wrong, I am not running down Manchester United because I think they are a very, very good side – a good footballing side, at that. It is just that teamwork won the title in the end which is so often the case.

"Even when people were happily writing off Leeds' chances of returning the title to Yorkshire for the first time since 1974, they stuck at it, they kept plugging away in the belief that they could still win it. They used their teamwork and their self-belief to sustain a challenge which, at times, looked to be faltering. They were helped along the way by many things, not least their supporters. If you go to Elland Road these days you know that you are guaranteed a wonderful atmosphere. It can be like a bear-pit in there sometimes, particularly under floodlights, and that really helps to lift players. It is a very intimidating place to go.

"You can put Manchester United's failure to win the title down to many things – the state of their Old Trafford pitch, fixture congestion, injuries etc etc – but I have always believed that, at the end of the day, the best team in the country wins the Championship. It is a very long and demanding season here in this country and the team which finishes on the top of the pile deserves to be there because they have shown greater consistency than anyone else. You just can't argue against that.

"Obviously, those sides who don't quite manage to sustain their level of consistency can proffer hard-luck stories but that has always happened in this sport and it will always happen. Every side can claim mitigating circumstances but, then again, the League Champions can also point to moments of ill-fortune. The big difference is that they can proudly say that they were the ones – the only ones – who managed successfully to overcome all the obstacles that were laid in their path during the course of a very lengthy campaign.

"I do feel some sympathy for Manchester United because they were the favourites, they were up near the top for the whole of the season and I know just how desperately they wanted to win that title. But, the fact of the matter is, they didn't stay the course while Leeds United did."

Kendall is convinced that Leeds will equip themselves well in the seasons ahead and he forecasts a bright future for a club he has long admired. "The fact that they will have set their hearts on successfully defending their title and will also have the additional challenge of trying to lift the European Cup will, I am sure, guarantee that the momentum is maintained next season.

"I must admit that I do envy them their chance of winning the European Cup because that was something which my team was twice denied during my first spell at Everton. We won the Championship in both 1985 and 1987 but because of the ban imposed after the tragedy at the Heysel Stadium we were banned from taking part. That was so disappointing because after you have proved yourselves to be the best at domestic level you are so anxious to go out and try and prove that you are also the best in Europe. I wish them well.

"I would love to say that I believe Leeds are well equipped for the extra special challenge of European football but perhaps I am not the best judge of that because I honestly thought Arsenal would do well this season and look what happened to them! Let's face it, Leeds are already a very, very good side so they will perhaps need to add only a couple of top-quality players during the summer. Howard will know the positions he wishes to strengthen and he will know he needs quality players.

"To be a successful manager you really do have to be utterly ruthless when the occasion demands. I remember the public reaction to my decision to buy Gary Lineker at the end of the 1984-85 season. We had won the Championship and the man who led our attack so brilliantly that season was Andy Gray. He was a genuine, 22-carat folk-hero at Goodison Park but, after securing Lineker, I sold him. Many Everton supporters just couldn't believe what I had done.

"The thing was, I was already looking to the future. You must always try and improve what you have got and that is what Howard will have to do. It may lead to a little unrest at terrace level if he decides to replace a firm favourite but, believe me, it has to be done. You can't stand still, you must plan ahead and move with the times.

Even if a new player improves your side by only a few per cent it is worth doing. Howard Wilkinson is a very good manager with great tactical awareness and a vision of exactly where it is he wants to take Leeds United. I don't think the club could be in better – or safer – hands.''

Howard Kendall gave me his assessment of the recognised 1991-92 Leeds United team.

JOHN LUKIC: ''One of my firm beliefs is that no team can even contemplate winning the League Championship unless they have an exceptional goalkeeper. If you look back down the years, I think you will find that each and every title-winning side has had a goalkeeper of great natural ability.

''Arsenal had David Seaman last season and John himself during the 1988-89 season, Liverpool have had Bruce Grobbelaar and before him Ray Clemence, and at Everton I had arguably the best of the lot in Neville Southall. It really is imperative that a team's defence has someone who is totally reliable standing behind them.

''John's big advantage was that he had done it all before during his time at Highbury; he had been down the Championship path once already and knew exactly what to expect and what was expected of him. There really is no substitute for experience in football and John has plenty of that. He is, without any shadow of a doubt, one of the best three of four goalkeepers in English football and it is more than a little surprising that he hasn't found himself more involved in the England international set-up. So, from the point of view of experience and general all-round ability, he was a wonderful signing.

''I know that many, many people raised their eyebrows when George Graham decided to allow him to leave Arsenal but he obviously believed that by selecting Seaman he was improving the quality of his first team. That is fair enough . . . there can be no better reason.

"John is big, strong and brave, and is a superb shot-stopper. Perhaps his most important quality is that he can command and organise those players who are directly in front of him. The Leeds defence trust him. If you look at the record books you will see that Leeds did not concede very many penalties during the course of their Championship season. The reason for that is the faith which defenders have in John's abilities. If an opposition forward does manage to break through the back-line why bring him down with a late, despairing challenge and risk giving away a spot kick? Why do that when there is a very good chance that your goalkeeper will leap to the rescue."

MEL STERLAND: "Mel is another player of vast experience who has, perhaps, surprised a great many people during the course of the past few months. He is what I would label a 'hungry' footballer, namely someone who has a tremendous appetite for winning the ball. He will never shirk a tackle, he will never place his own personal safety above the well-being of the team he is playing for. Aggressive and very, very strong, he is a genuine competitor in the Stuart Pearce mould.

"The other tremendous thing about having someone like him in your starting line-up is that you know, at the start of a season, he is going to weigh in with his fair share of goals. All players should mentally set themselves targets at the start of a campaign, whether they be playing in defence, midfield or attack. I am sure that most full-backs would gladly settle for two or three per season but you get the distinct impression that this lad wants about nine or ten. He is always willing to try his luck from any distance whether it be from a set-piece or from open play and that is such a valuable asset for any manager.

"The other important thing he brings to the Leeds team is his ability to cross a good ball from either flank. He must have been instrumental in creating 15 to 20 goals this season. Indeed, it was noticeable that Leeds' goals-per-game ratio dipped quite appreciably towards the end of the season after Mel had been ruled out following surgery. I have always liked dependable players and he is one of them."

TONY DORIGO: "I am a very big fan of Tony's: I think he is a quality footballer. At one point people seemed unsure whether he would ultimately make his mark at left-back or on the left side of midfield. With Leeds, because of the manner in which they play, he has been able to start off in defence yet make a significant, perhaps overlooked, contribution in the middle of the park as well.

"He is exceptionally quick and, like Sterland, he can deliver a very good cross to either the near or far post.

"It is a little unfortunate for him that Stuart Pearce has made the left-back spot very much his own in our national side. Graham Taylor must be absolutely delighted to have Tony as a more than able deputy.

"It could well be that Tony will end up being the Norman Hunter of his generation. Norman was a brilliant player but won only a limited number of caps because he was just behind Bobby Moore in the pecking order. It will be a great shame if that was to happen to Tony but if Leeds do continue to collect the major honours he won't be too downhearted."

CHRIS WHYTE: "I suppose that it is fair to say that his form has been one of the season's great revelations. I wouldn't say it has been any great surprise, certainly not to me at least, because he has always been a more than useful player.

"What has helped him enormously is having someone like Chris Fairclough alongside him. The two complement each other so very well and you would think, to look at them, they had been playing alongside each other for many, many years.

"He is quick, mobile, strong in the tackle and, quite naturally, very good in the air.

"He suffered many disappointments during the early part of his career but it has all come good for him now and I'm delighted for him because he is a good, honest, hard-working professional."

CHRIS FAIRCLOUGH: "His contribution to the Leeds defence is so similar to that of his partner, Chris Whyte, that I could just say, 'ditto, ditto'. When Howard Wilkinson bought him from Tottenham Hotspur, he was, in essence, rescuing him because a career which initially had promised so very much appeared to be on the verge of going sour.

"Like Whyte he is quick, diligent and naturally aggressive. He is one of Leeds' great unsung heroes and with youth on his side he could well be a mainstay of their defence for several years to come."

DAVID BATTY: "The biggest compliment I can pay this young man is to say that every team in the Football League would love to have a player of his ability on their staff.

"The great problem is that there are so few of his type around these days. Years ago it seemed that every club, whether they were in the First Division or the Fourth Division, had a player fashioned in the Batty mould – someone who could tackle tigerishly and then have enough skill to distribute the ball with authority and common sense. They do seem to be something of a dying breed which makes him all the more invaluable to Howard Wilkinson.

"He has many facets to his game – an ability to collect the ball, to sweep up, to inspire those around him, to set players free with one, well-driven pass from deep.

"At one point, not so long ago, it did seem highly probable that his natural enthusiasm and aggression would be his downfall. He did go through a spell where he was constantly falling foul of officials but the change in attitude over the past 18 months or so has been quite remarkable – and most welcome from Leeds' point of view.

"Much of the credit for Batty's new approach to football must go to his manager for he has calmed down yet he has not lost his cutting edge. He still desperately wants to win every ball and every tackle. He is a competitor and a winner. His only problem would seem to be finding the rear of the opponents' net but I am sure that his strike-rate will improve as he matures as a player.

"If I was to liken him to anybody then it would probably be Peter Reid. Need I say any more?"

GARY McALLISTER: "Technically, Gary is possibly a better player than is Batty but just like the relationship between Whyte and Fairclough, he has struck a really tremendous partnership with David at the heart of midfield.

"He has very good vision and I wasn't at all surprised to learn that he had won a place in the Professional Footballers' Association First Division team.

"He is actually quite tall for a midfield player and that is very much to his advantage because his physical presence helps him win the ball. Gary is a very talented footballer and his arrival at Elland Road was crucial to Leeds' development."

GARY SPEED: "He is another player whom I admire greatly. Gary must be one of the brightest talents in English football and certainly one of the most improved. He has developed at such a pace since his side won the Second Division Championship that he is now, although still young, almost the finished article.

"Apart from his natural turn of speed (no pun intended!) he is a tremendous crosser of the ball and also packs a very useful shot. The thing which people tend to overlook when discussing his skills is his heading ability which is terrific and one of the most potent weapons in the Leeds armoury.

"He is particularly useful at the back post for set-piece moves, whether it be corners or free-kicks. If a long ball is floated into the penalty area and drifts beyond the likes of Chapman and Wallace it will quite often find its way to either the head or feet of Speed.

"He is also a most versatile player as he proved towards the end of the season when he played several games at full-back. It must have been difficult for him to adapt to defensive duties bearing in mind his in-bred desire to push forward, but he certainly did not let anyone down. Terry Yorath must be deliriously happy that he was born in Wales because he seems destined for a glittering future for both club and country."

GORDON STRACHAN: "What a marvellous signing that was! What an inspired piece of business by Howard Wilkinson. To pick up a player of his quality and experience for just £300,000 was a bargain; a real steal. There is not a great deal I can say about Gordon that hasn't already been said and written a million and one times over the past couple of years. His move to Leeds totally rejuvenated his career at a time when he appeared to be heading down a blind alley at Manchester United. Alex Ferguson received a lot of stick for allowing him to leave Old Trafford but you have to remember that he was only doing what he believed was best for his club. It may well be that had Gordon stayed on the other side of the Pennines his career would have petered out prematurely. Sometimes footballers require a complete change of scenery if they are to prolong their careers and that was possibly the case on this occasion.

"Once Gordon arrived at Elland Road he started to play like an 18-year-old once again. He was, if you like, reborn despite the fact that Leeds were, at the time, languishing in the Second Division. The task of helping the club back towards the First Division – and then back to the very summit of English football – obviously appealed greatly to him.

"He is so comfortable on the ball and has the uncanny knack of popping up in the right place at the right time. He passes well, marshals the whole team superbly and motivates those working around him. He is a very, very intelligent player who can slow a game down when it needs to be slowed down and who can get things moving when the situation cries out for immediate action.

"There are very few real bargains to be had in football these days but Mr Wilkinson unearthed a real gem when he signed this man."

ROD WALLACE: "Rod is a player who is gifted with terrific speed and that alone is sufficient to make him a major threat to any defence. I don't think he is the most clinical of finishers but the fact that he can leave most defenders trailing over 20 or 30 yards means that he will always pick up between 10 and 15 goals per season.

"Although he does occasionally suffer from bouts of inconsistency he is a potential match-winner on his day as we at Everton found out to our cost during a Rumbelows Cup tie at Goodison Park back in December.

"Just as long as he is surrounded by quality players – as he is at Leeds – he will continue to improve."

LEE CHAPMAN: "I was at Stoke City when Lee began his career so I have watched his development with keen interest down the years. After making a name for himself in the Potteries, Lee was lured to Arsenal in 1982 in a £500,000 deal – a lot of money at the time. There is no doubt at all that he was wrong to move down to London because by joining such a big club at such a tender age, he unwittingly called a halt to his natural development as a player.

"Inevitably, things just didn't work out for him at Highbury and he seemed to play all over the place before finally ending up at Leeds United. I think that even Lee would be the first to acknowledge that he is not the most technically gifted of players but he more than compensates for this by working so hard in and around the penalty area. If he gets the right service he is one of the most proficient forwards in the First Division. His scoring record since joining Leeds is absolutely superb and stands comparison with the very best strikers in the English game."

ERIC CANTONA: "I haven't seen very much of this lad but he doesn't strike me as the 'superbrat' he is supposed to be. From what I can gather, he has settled into the swing of things very, very quickly and his decision to make permanent his move from France would suggest that he is very happy in Yorkshire.

"From what I have seen of him there is no doubt about his talent. It is difficult to say whether he will be able to hold down a regular first-team place on a week-to-week basis but even if he doesn't he is a very useful player to have in any squad.

"He seems to have a gift for the unorthodox and the indications are that he may well make the grade. It is sometimes difficult for 'foreign' players to settle in this country but he seems to have a nice, laid-back atttude to his life and to his work and that may well help him."

STEVE HODGE: "Another very useful player to have 'knocking on the door'. I have always admired players who will give 100 per cent every time they are selected and he is one of them.

"He is a very productive worker and he is always likely to snatch an important goal."

Chapter Six

"I DON'T BELIEVE IT . . ."
THE MANCHESTER UNITED TRILOGY

At the start of the season when Howard Wilkinson made clear that his primary objective was a final league position high enough to guarantee qualification for the UEFA Cup, he had said that "anything else would be a bonus". By his own admission he did not feel his senior squad to be strong enough to actually win the Championship itself so it would be logical to assume that the bonuses to which he was referring was one of the major cup competitions – any of the major cup competitions.

For all Leeds' tradition, the club had not won a major knock-out trophy since defeating Arsenal in the 1972 FA Cup final. The two decades which had elapsed since Allan Clarke's famous diving header had brought the famous old trophy to Elland Road for the first, and so far only, time were littered with moments of immense disappointment. Having reached the semi-finals of the Rumbelows League Cup in the previous season, Wilkinson was aware that the team which he had painstakingly constructed was as proficient at sudden-death football as it was at negotiating an arduous and demanding League programme.

Never a club to willingly reduce its options, Leeds had entered the Zenith Data Systems Cup – a much-maligned competition and one which several of the so-called "glamour" sides had declined to participate in for a variety of unfathomable reasons, the most salient of which was undoubtedly basic snobbery.

While Leeds' decision to compete in a tournament which is invariably low-key until the latter stages was welcomed by the sponsors, it would be fair to say that it did not feature too highly on the priority list of either manager or players.

For the second-round tie against Nottingham Forest at Elland Road Wilkinson, restricted by injuries, was forced to name a side which lacked Gordon Strachan, Gary McAllister and Lee Chapman. Although Rod Wallace climbed off the substitute's bench to score a fine goal, Leeds eventually succumbed to an enthusiastic Forest side, 3–1, before a crowd of just 6,495. It is doubtful whether too many tears of regret were shed behind the dressing-room doors.

Leeds' assault on the cup competitions had actually begun in late September when they were paired with Scunthorpe United in the second round of the Rumbelows Cup. The first leg at Glanford Park was a surprisingly tight and nervous affair as the Fourth Division minnows pursued the most unlikely of victories with great spirit and adventure. With the second leg at Elland Road always likely to decide the outcome, Leeds were not too disappointed with a goalless draw although they were possibly a little embarrassed at their failure to impose their collective will on an enthusiastic, but clearly inferior, side. Howard Wilkinson was celebrating the third anniversary of his arrival at the club on the night goals by Mel Sterland, Gary Speed and Lee Chapman finally put paid to Scunthorpe and moved Leeds forward into the competition's third round and a home tie against Tranmere Rovers.

Tranmere, for so long the Cinderella club of Merseyside football, were going well upon their long-anticipated return to the Second Division and with John Aldridge, the former Liverpool striker, scoring almost at will, they could not be treated lightly. Maximum respect was due and maximum respect was duly afforded a team which had rightly won a reputation for playing attacking football of the very highest order.

Rovers made life distinctly uncomfortable for Wilkinson's side and a surprisingly small crowd of just over 18,000 must have been grateful that the normally prolific and reliable Aldridge was enduring one of his less productive evenings. True, the Republic of Ireland international did eventually find his way on to the score sheet but ultimately Leeds were far too strong for worthy opponents and two goals by Lee Chapman and one by Carl Shutt guaranteed a place in the last 16 of a competition which Leeds had last won in 1968.

Leeds' reward for a performance which was workmanlike rather than inspired was a trip to Goodison Park to face Everton. Although the season was still very much in its infancy, the Merseysiders had lost their early impetus in the League programme and, subconsciously at least, they had isolated cup football as a possible route to success and salvation.

Irrespective of how Everton are faring, playing at Goodison Park in front of one of English football's most vociferous and knowledgeable audiences is not easy. It was an unenviable task but one which Leeds approached with typical enthusiasm and verve.

If nothing else this one game proved beyond a shadow of a doubt that Leeds was a team which had few equals in terms of in-bred, unshakeable confidence. Despite falling behind to a spectacular long-range strike by Ray Atteveld, the Dutch midfield player, Leeds did not panic, did not get flustered, did not change the emphasis of a game which was centred around the supremacy which David Batty and Gary McAllister were enjoying in a midfield section which was often overcrowded.

Although Everton did briefly threaten to add a second, possibly decisive, goal, Leeds held firm and slowly began to grasp the game by its throat. By the final whistle, the Leeds supporters must have been wondering what all the fuss had been about. Two goals by Rodney Wallace and incisive strikes by Lee Chapman and Gary Speed ensured a comfortable victory. The scoreline was not in the least bit misleading; it had been a rout.

Having moved forward into the quarter-finals, Wilkinson, privately at least, must have been optimistic about his side's chances of "going all the way" for many of the First Division's leading clubs had long since fallen by the wayside. Several unfancied sides had also laid claim to a place in the last eight and a sympathetic draw would almost certainly have seen Leeds installed as the competition's new favourites. Sadly, if predictably, the draw was not sympathetic – it was not even reasonably kind. It was arch-rivals and fellow title-chasers, Manchester United at home.

The pairing of English football's two most successful clubs was given extra spice as they were scheduled to contest a League fixture of obvious significance just ten days earlier at the same venue. Astonishingly, what was initially billed as the big showdown was to be transformed into a blockbusting saga of quite epic proportions when the draw for the third round of the FA Cup was made a few days later. Once again the two Uniteds were drawn together and once again Elland Road was the venue. It was a million to one chance and it rendered the supporters, players and managers of both clubs speechless.

"My first reaction was one of absolute disbelief. These things can happen in football but it just seemed ridiculous," said Alex Ferguson. The "trilogy", as it is popularly referred to, provoked unprecedented interest amongst the country's media. Television schedules were hastily rearranged so that all three games could be broadcast live to a fascinated nation and a posse of leading journalists headed for West Yorkshire to take up semi-permanent residence. The stage was set for three explosive fixtures in just 18 days. The whole country held its breath as the two heavyweights shaped up for a gruelling contest which was, in so many respects, to shape the entire season.

The gloves came off on 29 December when Manchester United arrived for the first instalment – the league game. It was fast, furious and frantic. No quarter was asked, none was surrendered.

Although Leeds enjoyed by far the better of the early chances they were unable to penetrate a defence which was superbly marshalled by the impressive Gary Pallister. After dominating for long spells, Leeds fell behind to a Neil Webb goal. As both time and patience began to run out, there was good reason for concern. The title was on the verge of slipping away.

As the game entered its final few minutes and at a time when the visitors had unashamedly fallen back to defend their slender advantage, Pallister blotted his copy-book when he foolishly brought Gary McAllister crashing down just inside the penalty area. Mel Sterland, a man who often gives the distinct impression that he had his central nervous system removed shortly after birth, stepped forward to drive the resulting spot-kick beyond the reach of the despairing Peter Schmeichel. Leeds had squared the match, secured a priceless point and, in terms of the title's destiny, posed more questions than they had answered.

Episode two of football's equivalent of a soap opera came on 8 January when the clubs met to contest a place in the semi-finals of the Rumbelows Cup. This time there were to be no arguments; Manchester United played superbly and, as both managers were later to concede their winning margin of 3-1 was in no way flattering.

The final instalment followed just seven days later, this time in the FA Cup. The term, "travesty of justice" is often used in conjunction with sporting events, par-ticularly football. It is often misused; it is often totally inappropriate. On this occasion not only was it the most apt of phrases – it was the *only* suitable phrase. Not to put too fine a point on it, Leeds played their great rivals off the park. But for the athletic brilliance of Schmeichel – that and some distinctly poor finishing by the Leeds forwards – the game, as a competition, would have been effectively over long before the half-time interval.

Unfortunately, Leeds would have struggled to hit a barn door from six yards on the day. Chapman, Wallace, Speed and McAllister all squandered chances which ranged from the difficult to the simple. It was not be. Having soaked up an enormous amount of pressure, Manchester United, to their immense credit, broke free down the left flank. Ryan Giggs crossed from the by-line and Mark Hughes applied the finishing touch with a firm, downwards header.

Worse was to follow for Leeds. In a last desperate bid to rescue the game, Chapman bravely threw himself for-ward in a forlorn attempt to reach a near-post cross. His sense of balance betrayed him at the crucial moment and his left wrist crumpled under the shuddering impact. He was led away to the dressing-room and out of Leeds' season for six weeks.

With the benefit of hindsight, many people picked out the "trilogy" as the turning point for both Leeds United and for Manchester United. Elimination from the two major cup competitions left Leeds free to concentrate on the Championship; victory left Manchester United with far too much to do. Eventually, they were to pay a very high price for their own success.

Gary McAllister comments: "Once we had moved through into the quarter-finals of the Rumbelows Cup, and once we knew that Manchester United had also won their way through into the last eight, we knew that we would be drawn against them. It was just a feeling within the dressing-room. Sometimes you think that certain things are just meant to be and that was one of them. Obviously, the good thing about it was that we had come out of the hat first. It is a cliché, but it is true to say that all you can hope for in cup football is a home draw. We knew that Manchester United would not relish coming to Elland Road.

"Like everyone else within football, I really could not believe the draw for the third round of the FA Cup when it was announced. It was such a crazy coincidence that it seemed impossible. I don't know what the odds were against the two clubs being paired in both the competitions but they must have been astronomical. It was almost too much to take in. Again, the saving grace was the fact that we would once more be at home. The first of the three games, the League fixture, was a really cracking affair which could have gone either way. Looking back now, I would say that a draw was just about right. At one point it didn't look like we were going to take anything from that game because once we had missed a number of chances, and once they had got their noses in front, I knew it was going to be difficult to get back on level terms. I am sure that they would have settled for a point beforehand so once they took the lead it was pretty obvious that they were going to fall back in numbers and try and hang on. It would have probably ended in defeat for us had Gary Pallister not clattered into me as I chased a through ball in the penalty area.

"That was a crucial result for us because, at the time, Manchester United were above us in the table and had they extended their advantage they would have grown in confidence. We desperately needed that point. The Rumbelows Cup tie was a different ball game altogether. They absolutely battered us in that one. They thoroughly deserved to win and the final scoreline of 3-1 might have been painful from our point of view but I do believe that it was a true reflection of how the tie had gone.

"I don't think it was that we played that badly on the day – they were just superb. It was their two wide men, Ryan Giggs and Andrei Kanchelskis, who made all the difference. They made life really uncomfortable for our defence.

"To say that we were unlucky in the FA Cup tie would be an understatement. It was just one of those dreadful days when we couldn't find the net. We did everything else that was required of us throughout the 90 minutes but try as we might, we just couldn't score. We couldn't really have gone closer to scoring – having shots brilliantly saved or kicked off the line – but it wouldn't go in. That happens sometimes. Maybe it's fate. The fact that you know you have played extremely well and still lost makes it even harder to accept. We were all feeling very, very low afterwards because we knew that a great opportunity to make progress had gone.

"I think even the players of Manchester United would admit that they were exceedingly fortunate to win that one. We put them under so much pressure that they were almost totally reliant upon breakaways. They made one of those counter-attacks pay, though, when Giggs raced clear down the left and delivered that inch-perfect cross for Mark Hughes. It was a bad day all round because we lost Lee Chapman with a very serious wrist injury.

"However, they say that every cloud has a silver lining and after the season was finally over I think we all realised that was perfectly true. I really do think that being knocked out of the two major cup competitions at such an early stage was a blessing in disguise. We didn't feel that way at the time but I think that it is fair to say that Manchester United actually did us a big favour.

"It meant that with almost four months of the season left to run, we only had one thing left to aim for. We started the season with four targets but we now had only one left. The consolation was that the only thing which we could now go on and win was the biggest prize of them all – the League Championship. It made us all the more determined to stick at it and keep collecting as many points as was possible.

"The trilogy of games against Manchester United was very demanding and, in the end, rather disappointing from our point but I do believe that it could have been instrumental in us going on to win the title.

"In the previous year, we had suffered from a very bad fixture pile-up towards the end of the season because we were involved in the latter stages of both the Rumbelows Cup and the Zenith Data Systems Cup. We knew what sort of toll it had taken on us and we suspected that it might do the same to Manchester United. As things turned out, that is precisely what happened. Just as we had been forced into a situation where we were expected to play four, very important, games in just six days, so too were our rivals from Old Trafford. It doesn't matter how well you are going at the time or how good a team you are, that is just too much to ask. It is far too demanding for even the most accomplished of sides.

"I knew that if Manchester United were faced by a congested programme towards the end of the season, we would have a great chance of pipping them in the League. So it turned out."

The view that Manchester United unwittingly handed Leeds the initiative in the League by removing them from the cup competitions is now widely supported.

"There can be no doubt that Manchester United helped Leeds' cause by winning those two cup-ties," says Ron Atkinson, the manager of Aston Villa. "Fixture congestion, whether it be early in the season or towards the end of the campaign, is a real killer.

"If you are faced by a situation where you have several important games in the space of just a few days, it really does sap the strength of even the fittest player. It is ironic that Manchester United should ultimately pay a very high price for their own success. Things would possibly have been very different on the League front had Leeds won either of those cup ties. As it was they were left free to focus all their attentions on the Championship.

"They were not hampered by endless midweek fixtures. While their closest rivals were out fighting tooth and nail in the cups, the players of Leeds were relaxing and conserving their energy. That was a crucial factor in their success."

Manchester City manager, Peter Reid, is another seasoned professional who subscribes to the same viewpoint. "I remember from my days at Everton back in the mid-Eighties just how many problems success can bring. It just doesn't seem fair somehow that the better you are – the more games you win – the bigger the price you end up paying," he said.

"Although Alex Ferguson and his players will have felt a great sense of jubilation after winning at Elland Road in the Rumbelows Cup and in the FA Cup, I think they might somehow regret those victories a little now. Of course, you can't turn around and say that Manchester United would have gone on to win the League title had they lost those two games because that just would not be fair on Leeds United. It might well have been a totally different story but we will never know."

Chapter Seven

GOODBYE UNCERTAINTY, BONJOUR ERIC

If Howard Wilkinson did commit himself to a New Year's resolution as he bid a fond farewell to 1991, it would almost certainly have had its roots in his season-long desire to give his club's supporters tangible evidence of a transformation which was beginning to gather pace. As Leeds prepared for the game against struggling West Ham United at Upton Park on the opening day of 1992, they were lying in second place, trailing Manchester United by a solitary point. Twenty-four hours later, somewhat improbably, they were back on top of the First Division, one point clear of their fiercest rivals.

West Ham, famed for their puritanical approach to football, were already embroiled in a desperate fight against relegation, one which was to end in failure. The game turned out to be something of a personal triumph for Lee Chapman who scored twice during the course of an emphatic 3–1 victory – his first League goals in more than a month.

With the kick-off of Manchester United's game against Queen's Park Rangers at Old Trafford delayed until the evening to accommodate a live television broadcast, Leeds moved back to the summit of the First Division. Bearing in mind the erratic form of a QPR side which was prone to lapses of concentration when playing away from Loftus Road, most people assumed that the positions would once again be reversed come 9.30 pm.

Remarkably, Rangers produced a performance of astonishing maturity in the most intimidating of circumstances. At the conclusion of a match which was totally

71

one-sided – in favour of the visitors – sections of the 38,000 crowd vented their anger and their disgust. Manchester United had not just been beaten 4–1, they had been humiliated. The cracks had begun to show. It was the first indication that Alex Ferguson's glorious dream was on the verge of being turned into a waking nightmare.

Whilst a meeting with old rivals Sheffield Wednesday at Hillsborough could hardly be described as ideal when the leadership of the First Division is at stake, Leeds travelled down to South Yorkshire for their next game in buoyant and confident mood. All along they had been told that Manchester United's installation as champions was little more than a formality. Each and every time they dropped points they were informed that their rivals' games in hand would prove to be the decisive factor and yet Queen's Park Rangers had prised open the doors which led to the Promised Land. With just over three months of the season left to run, suddenly anything – and everything – seemed possible.

Predictably, the game at Hillsborough was shown live on television, Gary McAllister's belief that he and his team-mates were "switched on" by the presence of the cameras was lent more credence in the most amazing fashion.

Four days earlier, Leeds' season seemed to be lurching towards potential disaster after the emphatic Rumbelows Cup defeat at Elland Road. Howard Wilkinson, back at the club where he made his name, demanded a display of character and resilience to silence the many critics who were lining up to write off his team as also-rans. The response was staggering.

At the end of what was arguably Leeds United's finest performance in more than 15 years, Wednesday had been humbled, 6–1. It was a day of magnificent football, great goals, lavish entertainment and memorable milestones. Lee Chapman's brilliant hat-trick was the first by a Leeds player away from Elland Road in more than 12 years. Mel Sterland was playing at Hillsborough for the first time since he left Wednesday to join Glasgow Rangers three years earlier. John Lukic chalked up his

Steve Hodge sweeps home the late equaliser in the 1—1 draw against Sheffield Wednesday at Elland Road, 24 August 1991

Lee Chapman outjumps Gary Pallister to head home Leeds' goal in the 1—1 draw against championship rivals Manchester United at Old Trafford, 31 August 1991

Steve Hodge's goal gives Leeds victory over Liverpool for the first time in 18 years, 21 September 1991

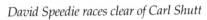

David Speedie races clear of Carl Shutt

Lee Chapman heads home the fourth goal in the 4—1 demolition of Aston Villa at Villa Park, 24 November 1991

Something of a rarity . . . Mel Sterland loses out to Oldham's Paul Bernard, 26 October 1991

Rod Wallace fires home the late winner against Everton at Elland Road, 30 November 1991

Mel Sterland's penalty rescues an invaluable point in the league game against Manchester United at Elland Road, 29 December 1991

Lee Chapman scores Leeds' third goal in the 3—1 victory over West Ham United at Upton Park, 1 January 1992

Before the storm . . .Gary Speed celebrates his goal in the 3—1 Rumbelows Cup defeat by Manchester United at Elland Road, 8 January 1992

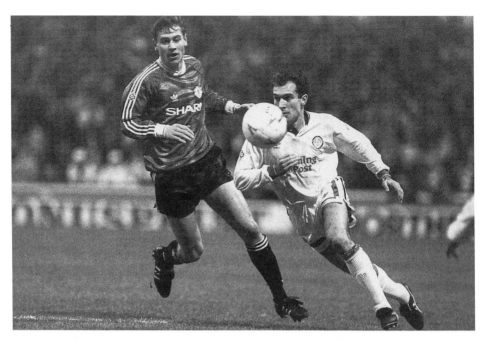

*Tony Dorigo dispossesses Andrei Kanchelskis of Manchester United during the
Rumbelows Cup tie at Elland Road, 8 January 1992*

*Putting the owls to flight. Lee Chapman celebrates one of his three goals in the
6—1 win over Sheffield Wednesday at Hillsborough, 12 January 1992*

Le Crunch . . . Crystal Palace goalkeeper Nigel Martyn feels the full force of Gary McAllister's challenge, 18 January 1992

Lee Chapman scores in the 6—1 victory over Sheffield Wednesday at Hillsborough, 12 January 1992

No entry . . . Crystal Palace's Thorn halts the progress of Carl Shutt during the drawn League game at Elland Road, 18 January 1992

250th senior appearance for Leeds since his transfer from Arsenal and Chris Whyte the 250th of his career.

The victory sent shock waves rippling through the English game. Those who had previously dismissed Leeds' challenge as either lightweight or lacking in any real substance swiftly modified their opinion and changed their stance. These so-called experts, these people of little faith, finally began to peer anxiously through the veil of suspicion which had descended earlier in the season to calmly announce that, yes, Leeds *were* a fine footballing team and, yes, the possibility of the Championship returning to Elland Road was not quite as ludicrous as it had once seemed.

Clive White, the respected *Times* journalist, did not hesitate to describe Leeds' performance against Sheffield Wednesday as "the finest display of attacking football seen within the Football League all season". It was an unerringly accurate appraisal.

Gary McAllister summed it up: "The performance at Sheffield Wednesday was one of the finest I have ever been involved in. Just as we had done against Aston Villa earlier in the season, we just clicked – everything went beautifully and we were enjoying ourselves so much out there that we would have played all afternoon and all night if the referee had let us. If I am perfectly honest I have to admit that, in the end, it did become a little embarrassing because we were battering them and they simply could not cope. Even when they had slightly pegged us back with what was not so much a controversial penalty as a ridiculous penalty, we kept playing neat, productive football. It was one of those games where we fancied ourselves to score every time we crossed the half-way line. When you hit your form like we did that afternoon there is very little the opposition can do about it. Wednesday, although they tried very hard, couldn't halt us. I doubt any side in the country could have handled us on that day. We were hot and we knew it.

"After the bitter disappointment of going out of the Rumbelows Cup to Manchester United in front of our own supporters, it really was the near-perfect way in which to bounce back. After a bad defeat, you are always

73

anxious to get into another match to get things well and truly out of your system. Sometimes the next game goes well, sometimes it doesn't. This time it went perfectly.

"To start the new year with maximum points from two away games which, on paper at least, were a little bit tricky was a marvellous boost for us. It really set us up for the coming weeks. We could have asked for no more than to win two games and to score nine goals, away from home, in the process."

January's final League fixture, curiously on the 18th of the month, was something of an anti-climax. The Lord Mayor's show had most definitely left town and it took Chris Fairclough's first goal of the season to ensure a point was taken from the home game against an inconsistent Crystal Palace side. Fortunately, Manchester United were unable to capitalise and their failure to defeat lowly Notts County at Meadow Lane on the same afternoon ensured that Leeds remained in pole position on goal difference.

Top of the First Division at the end of January:

1. Leeds United	P 27	W 15	D 11	L 1	Pts 56
2. Manchester United	P 26	W 16	D 8	L 2	Pts 56

A comfortable 3–0 victory over Notts County at Elland Road on the first day of February strengthened Leeds' position at the top after Manchester United failed to defeat last season's champions, Arsenal, at Highbury. The win, which featured a rare, but nonetheless stunning, goal from David Batty, extended the club's unbeaten sequence to 16 games – the best since Howard Wilkinson arrived at the club. After becoming the first Division One side to score 50 goals, Leeds could justifiably claim to be one of the most attractive outfits in the entire Football League.

Having already lost the services of Lee Chapman, Leeds suffered another massive body-blow when Mel Sterland badly damaged an ankle. Although he battled on bravely – aided by pain-killing injections – he finally succumbed to the inevitable five weeks later and entered hospital for an operation which officially curtailed his season.

When Howard Wilkinson arrived to meet the assembled media after the defeat of Notts County, the talk was not of goals or championships but of a foreign footballer with a reputation for erratic, non-conformist behaviour. To the astonishment of those present, Wilkinson confirmed mounting speculation that Eric Cantona, the *enfant terrible* of French football, had officially put pen to paper and joined Leeds on loan. It was the final chapter in a curious story which first began in late January when Sheffield Wednesday manager, Trevor Francis, was seeking to secure a replacement for David Hirst, the England international forward who had sustained a serious injury. Unable to find a suitable player in this country, Francis had switched his attentions to the vast Continental market and had been told that the individual who met his requirements was Cantona. The problem was that the volatile superstar had only recently announced his retirement from professional football after receiving a lengthy suspension for arguing with a French Football Association disciplinary committee.

Cantona, who owns a sports newspaper in his native country and who spends much of his spare time either writing poetry or painting, said that he had absolutely no intention of playing again. His club, Nîmes, continued to hold his registration for purely legal reasons and after being approached by Francis they gave permission for informal negotiations to commence. After a couple of days of hard bargaining, Cantona announced that he had agreed to join Wednesday on loan for a brief period and that he would possibly make the move on a permanent basis if he found English football to his liking. Francis, aware that he was dealing with an unpredictable and unknown commodity, was equally cautious about Cantona's long-term future, saying only that he wanted to take a good look at the player during training.

While Francis's logic was unquestionably sound, he had, however, neglected to look at the weather forecast. It was mid-winter, his club's training pitch was frozen solid and there was no prospect of a thaw. Although Francis was able to study Cantona's skills on an artificial surface he was not convinced of the player's suitability.

Although Francis did name Cantona in his provisional squad for the game against Luton Town at Hillsborough on 1 February, he said that he was not prepared to offer the Frenchman any sort of contract until he had seen him perform on grass. He offered to extend the previously agreed loan period by another fortnight but Cantona refused, saying that he was a player of experience and that he did not need to prove himself to anyone. Rumour would have it that by the time the news of Cantona's Wednesday walk-out leaked out of Hillsborough, he was already ensconced in a Leeds hotel discussing the possibility of transferring his affections to Yorkshire's other leading club.

Wilkinson admitted that his interest in Cantona was not merely prompted by his sudden, unexpected availability and that he had long been aware of the player's unique talent. In fact, the Leeds manager confessed that he had already spoken to several people – including Glenn Hoddle – in a bid to gauge professional opinion about his would-be recruit.

Before Wednesday could attempt to resurrect their deal, Cantona was a Leeds United player – signed on loan until the end of the season. Little did he know that within a matter of a few weeks he would become the club's latest idol – and one of its most valuable assets.

Although Cantona was hindered by his limited command of English, his new team-mates and an expectant local public would soon discover – as the player himself had long insisted – that football is a universal language: a common currency. As if to establish an immediate bond between himself and his new club, Cantona pledged his future to Leeds United by insisting that he would never again play football in France. If he was to maintain the form he displayed towards the end of last season, very few would complain were he to finish his career at Elland Road.

If nothing else, Cantona's unexpected arrival provided the national press with countless stories as his somewhat controversial past was raked up, sifted through and analysed by a host of sporting celebrities. Terry Yorath, a key member of Leeds' Championship-winning side of 1974 and now the manager of the Welsh national team, believes that the signing of Cantona was, in some respects, a masterstroke on the part of Howard Wilkinson. "I'll tell you something, although Eric Cantona was to only make a limited number of appearances for the first team after his arrival, I honestly believe that he was one of the major reasons Leeds, and not Manchester United, went on to take the League title," he says.

"Of course Howard took a massive gamble even by taking the lad on extended loan. He arrived at Leeds with something of a reputation as a sporting hell-raiser and had he lived up to that reputation he could have caused untold damage. However, the gamble paid off handsomely. Eric arrived, behaved himself and blended in very, very quickly.

"When Leeds signed Cantona they signed much more than a mere footballer, they signed a man who had a certain magic about him. True, this air of mystery could be attributed to the fact that he was supposed to be the bad boy of French football. The thing is, supporters do like players who have a reputation. They seem to take to them straight away. I don't know what it is, perhaps they can identify with them.

"The other advantage was that Eric Cantona was a foreigner in a strange country. He couldn't speak the language, he was something of an innocent abroad. When someone like that turns up in your midst, the locals will always go out of their way to make him feel welcome. They want him to feel part of their club from the very moment he steps through the front door.

"Cantona seemed genuinely surprised by the warmth of the welcome which was afforded to him but that was because he didn't fully appreciate what the people of Yorkshire are like. They can be aggressive and single-minded, they can be blunt to the point of rudeness, but deep down inside they are a caring people who love nothing better than to push the boat out in an attempt to make a visitor feel welcome.

"Cantona arrived at exactly the right time. Maybe it was a conscious decision by Howard, maybe it wasn't. Although Leeds were still very much in contention for the Championship, they were being written off on a daily basis and the pressure was beginning to mount slowly. His arrival sparked the crowd back into life. It was like a breath of fresh air blowing through a dark and dusty room. There was genuine excitement out on the terraces. People stood around, clutching their programmes, awaiting news of the team selection. They were all silently praying he had been picked.

"You can't buy that sort of thing nor can you successfully appeal for it irrespective of who you are. I witness the same thing when Wales play international matches. When the news that people like Ian Rush and Mark Hughes are playing is broadcast over the public address system, you can sense the relief amongst the supporters.

"Not only did he lift the fans, I am almost certain he will also have lifted the players at what was a very crucial stage in the season. From a psychological point of view, his signing was so very important.

"I am not saying that Cantona will have a long and successful future within the Football League because I haven't seen enough of him to formulate a firm opinion. What I am saying is that even if he was to leave Leeds United next week, he has already played a significant part in the club's history. He is assured of hero-status no matter what he does or what he achieves in the years ahead.

"It is a very long time since Leeds United had a real cult hero. I couldn't, in all honesty, place Vinny Jones in that bracket although he too played his part during his brief spell at Elland Road. Excellent though the current Leeds team is, it didn't have a real star – a celebrity – until Cantona turned up. Liverpool have the likes of Rush, Bruce Grobbelaar and John Barnes, Manchester United have Hughes and Ryan Giggs, but Leeds didn't have one. They have now, though.

"Cantona is one of those rare individuals who is totally unorthodox. He has tremendous natural ability and great flair. I think we may find Howard using him next season much as he did this season, that is to say as a substitute or as a replacement for an injured colleague.

If that is the case, and if Cantona can adjust to life without a regular first-team place, I think he will continue to prosper.

"If I had to pick one, lasting memory of the 1991–92 season it would involve Cantona and that says a great deal about the impact he has already made. Of course, it was that wonderful goal against Chelsea when he hooked the ball over the head of a defender, established control and then flashed a volley into the roof of the net. As Cantona wheeled away to soak up the adulation of the Kop, my head fell to my knees. I hadn't seen a piece of skill like that for years. It was a truly unforgettable moment."

As the game against Oldham Athletic at Boundary Park began to draw ever nearer, the question of Cantona's possible inclusion became the sole topic of conversation in the pubs and clubs of Leeds. On the morning of the game, a party of 20 French journalists arrived in Oldham in the hope that their prodigal son would be included in the Leeds team. He wasn't, but he was given a place on the substitute's bench alongside Mike Whitlow. Ironically, his introduction to English football was to coincide with only Leeds' second League defeat of the season.

It was the sort of day which all footballers secretly dread – the day when little, or nothing, goes right. For once, Leeds were totally outplayed by opponents whose basic will to win seemed to be a good deal stronger. Oldham were quicker to the ball, more incisive when in possession and more ruthless in front of goal. They took their chances, Leeds did not and the final scoreline of 2–0 did not unduly flatter the hosts. Cantona did take to the field as a second-half substitute for Steve Hodge but Boundary Park was no place for graceful football and like so many of his colleagues he was a largely anonymous figure pursuing a painful exercise in damage limitation.

Gary McAllister reflects: "I still can't quite put my finger on what exactly happened to us at Oldham. For some reason they were fired up a great deal more than we were and that was reflected in the balance of play. It was just one of those afternoons when we couldn't get going at all. It didn't seem to matter what we tried, it just didn't come off for us. Afterwards, we had no real complaints at all because they fully deserved to win. In the end, they beat us quite comfortably. They held sway in every department; in every section of the pitch. It was one of our poorest performances of the season.

"Eric made his bow in English football that day and he must have been wondering what he had let himself in for. We went into the game on the top of the table but we never once played like prospective champions. He tried his best but it was asking too much to expect him to come off the bench and rescue a match which had already slipped away from our grasp."

Although Manchester United could only manage a draw against Sheffield Wednesday at Old Trafford on the same afternoon, it was sufficient to return them to the top of the First Division. Having surrendered the leadership with only the merest hint of defiance, Leeds' next fixture – against Everton at Goodison Park – could scarcely have been more demanding. Once again Wilkinson's team was ushered forward into the spotlight as a television audience gathered on a Sunday afternoon to closely monitor Leeds' response to a small crisis which so many confidently expected to be transformed into a genuine drama.

Twenty-four hours before Leeds took to the field of play on Merseyside, Manchester United had strengthened their position at the top by defeating Crystal Palace. The heat was on and the pressure was mounting. It was vitally important that Leeds did not lose to an Everton side which had begun to show the first, flickering signs of a mid-season revival in form. Many insisted that victory was essential but Wilkinson is a man who has always believed that the seizure of one point at certain venues – Goodison Park included – is tantamount to success. Although a goal by substitute Carl Shutt promised to give Leeds a morale-boosting victory, one moment of defensive slackness was to undermine an otherwise tidy performance. Matt Jackson's first-ever goal for Everton was sufficient to guarantee that the game ended all-square.

Having made his full debut at Goodison Park, Cantona was promptly relegated to the substitute's bench the following weekend when Luton Town arrived at Elland Road to continue their perennial fight against relegation to the Second Division. Cantona was demoted to accommodate the return of Lee Chapman who, despite being absent for seven weeks, had missed only five games. Inevitably, the prolific marksman was quick to make up for lost time and scored one of the goals in a 2–0 victory which wasn't quite as comfortable as the final scoreline might suggest.

The other scorer was Cantona who was hardly able to contain his delight after hooking the ball into the net following his introduction as a replacement for Tony Dorigo. As the Leeds supporters were soon to learn, no one celebrates a moment of glory quite like the Frenchman.

Top of the First Division at the end of February:

1. Manchester United	P 30	W 17	D 11	L 2	Pts 62
2. Leeds United	P 30	W 16	D 12	L 2	Pts 60

Gary McAllister recalls: "After losing at Oldham – and losing the leadership of the Division – we knew full well that we needed a good, solid performance at Goodison Park. Travelling to face a team like Everton is never particularly easy because even when they are struggling, their home record is usually very impressive.

"We were disappointed to only collect the one point because we played well and, perhaps, should have held on after Carl's deflected shot had given us a lead which we just about deserved. Just as Oldham had been, Everton were really fired up for that game. I suppose that is one of the problems of being near the top of the table – everybody wants to beat you; everybody seems to try that little bit harder against you.

"Some players will also tell you that playing on live television does bring a little extra pressure but it is something which you quickly get used to. If you are doing well then it is almost certain that several of your more important games are going to be selected for a live broadcast. Luton Town actually played very well at

Elland Road and many people must have wondered why it was they were struggling near the foot of the table. It was good to have Lee back in the side and it was good to see Eric claim his first goal for the club. The smile which illuminated his face after the ball had crossed the line told its own story. He was absolutely delighted and we were delighted for him."

With Manchester United involved in a Rumbelows Cup semi-final tie against Second Division Middlesbrough, Leeds had a glorious opportunity to reclaim pole position on 3 March when an Aston Villa side whose season had been prematurely ended arrived at Elland Road.

Leeds, uncharacteristically nervous, failed to play to their real potential and it was the visitors who were to enjoy the better chances in a fascinating game which swung first one way, then the other. The pace of Villa's Dalian Atkinson was a constant source of discomfort for the Leeds defence and the big striker appeared to have given his side the lead when he broke clear down the centre of the pitch before despatching a firm, low drive beyond the stranded John Lukic. Amazingly, the goal was ruled out either for offside or for an earlier, unseen, infringement. It was a stroke of good fortune for Leeds but one which they were unable to build upon.

As the match entered its final quarter, Leeds were awarded a controversial and highly dubious penalty. One point seemed destined to be magically transformed into three until Nigel Spink threw himself down to his left to save Gordon Strachan's spot-kick which, in truth, was both under-hit and badly directed. Victory had gone – and quite possibly the League Championship with it.

However, bouncing back in style had become something of a habit at Elland Road and four days later the captain's momentary indiscretion was forgotten when Tottenham Hotspur were reduced to rubble by a hugely convincing performance at White Hart Lane. After a season of persistent injury problems, Jon Newsome finally enjoyed a moment of personal satisfaction when he claimed his first senior goal of the campaign to add to strikes by Rod Wallace and Gary McAllister.

With their closest rivals inactive, Leeds returned to the top of the table to once again confound those critics who had declared their interest in the destiny of the title to be of a purely cursory nature.

But on the night that Manchester United were to clinch a place alongside Nottingham Forest in the Rumbelows Cup final by finally overcoming the spirited challenge of Middlesbrough, Leeds' sprint towards the great marathon's finishing line was rudely interrupted by a stumble of potentially calamitous proportions.

Although the form of Queen's Park Rangers had picked up appreciably in the previous three weeks, they were still widely regarded as a team of indifferent quality. True, they had destroyed Manchester United at Old Trafford on New Year's Day but even so they were not expected to pose too many problems despite enjoying home advantage.

For a while everything appeared to be running smoothly and going to plan. Leeds, as they usually did on their travels, were spraying the ball around nicely and with Gary McAllister and David Batty dominating in central midfield an evening devoid of problems seemed assured. Gary Speed pounced to give Leeds a deserved lead and then . . . collapse. Four times Rangers successfully breached Leeds' hitherto rock-solid defence. There was to be no defiant come-back. For once, Leeds had been outplayed.

Gary McAllister remembers: "Our form seemed to start fluctuating around this point in the season. One minute we were playing well, the next we were playing poorly.

"Although we missed a penalty during the game against Aston Villa, we didn't perform well. Villa had several really good chances and could have won. It would have been a case of rough justice had they actually lost – as they might have done – because they did ever so well and impressed me.

"I will always look back on the game against Tottenham with a sense of satisfaction because the team, as a whole, played well and I scored one of our three goals. People had been saying that a Leeds victory was something of a certainty because Spurs had lost so many of their home games but nothing is ever certain in football.

Had we not applied ourselves well to the job in hand, I doubt that we would have collected all three points on offer.

"On paper the result against Queen's Park Rangers looks absolutely dreadful but we did not deserve to lose by such a wide margin – no way. Loftus Road has proved to be a difficult ground for Leeds United in recent years even though we recorded an excellent victory there in a cup-tie last season. It was actually a good deal closer than it might look because Rangers scored a couple of late goals to give the false impression that we had been on the end of a real mauling.

"Although we were not picking up as many points as we had been hoping for, and although our level of consistency had dropped a little, we were still very optimistic about our chances at this stage. That might sound like a rather strange thing to say because I think I am right in saying that Manchester United were above us in the table and they had crucial games in hand.

"Because the title was effectively out of our own hands, we did keep looking for Manchester United's results. We had to because we knew that if they didn't falter there was no way we could win the Championship even if we were to win all our remaining fixtures. It was a difficult sort of phase for us because no matter what we did, we just didn't seem to be able to make up any ground on them. We kept picking up the points but the gap seemed to stay the same.

"It was a case of carrying on as best we could and concentrating on our own game. If United had won all their remaining games they would have thoroughly deserved to be champions and I would have been among the first to congratulate them. Our hope was that they would find they had bitten off more than they could chew and that the backlog would eventually hamper their progress."

Chapter Eight

THE RETURN TO GLORY

Against all expectations, with just nine League games remaining, Leeds United were still sitting proudly on top of the First Division table. When the wheat has been well and truly sorted from the chaff and there are just two teams left to seriously contest the League Championship most people would readily agree that it is not so much about performances or skill as sheer nerve.

As the great race began to enter its final few laps the same question was repeatedly asked of both the leading protagonists – do you have the bottle? It was a question to which Leeds had the perfect response, a response which the players of Manchester United attempted to duplicate but one which was to stick in their throats after a moment's fatal hesitation.

Typically, Howard Wilkinson went about his business as if his side was struggling in mid-table. He was asked on numerous occasions to forecast the final outcome of what had become one of the most intriguing Championship duels in living memory but he saw no reason to change a diplomatic stance which had served him well since late August. His usual answer, irrespective of the occasion, was: "There is still a long way to go; so much could happen to either team in the weeks ahead." Whether or not Wilkinson actually believed that his team was capable of negotiating a decidedly tricky end-of-term programme to lay claim to the big prize we shall never know but his public persona was that of a man completely at peace with both himself and his players.

On 14 March Leeds played host to Wimbledon whilst Manchester United were pitted against a revitalised Sheffield United at Bramall Lane. Naturally, both teams were expected to win but Leeds were wary of their visitors' reputation for not only gate-crashing private parties but also making a nuisance of themselves in the process.

If Wilkinson and his team were fearing an upset which could have shifted the balance of power, perhaps irretrievably, in Manchester United's favour, they were wrong. For once, Wimbledon behaved impeccably. Not only that, they did the decent thing and allowed the Leeds forward line to run amok and so improve, quite substantially, the club's already superior goal difference. A hat-trick by Lee Chapman and further goals by Eric Cantona and Rod Wallace serve to underline the cavernous gulf in class between the two sides. A very high percentage of the near-27,000 crowd remained behind on the final whistle to await the result from Bramall Lane. Sadly, despite being outplayed for lengthy periods, Manchester United had won, 2–1, to keep up their challenge and to increase the pressure.

The following weekend was, in so many respects, the acid test for Leeds – a televised game against defending champions, Arsenal, at Highbury. Playing Arsenal on their own territory is an unenviable task at the best of times but this was quite definitely not the best of times as the Gunners had launched a dramatic, belated bid to retain their title.

If Leeds needed an extra incentive to remind the watching millions of their Championship credentials it had arrived 24 hours earlier when Manchester United's increasing anxiety had manifested itself in a dismal performance against, of all people, Wimbledon. The side which had crumbled in such spectacular fashion at Elland Road just seven days earlier had stunned Old Trafford by holding out for a goalless draw. Indeed, had Terry Phelan, the former Leeds defender, not missed the simplest of chances in the dying seconds, United would have been condemned to the most embarrassing of defeats.

Although the game at Highbury failed to live up to expectations, Leeds seemed on course for a crucial victory when Lee Chapman claimed an opportunist goal, but a late equaliser by Paul Merson deservedly restored the status quo.

Gary McAllister says: "The Wimbledon result gave us a real boost – a real shot in the arm – because not only did we pick up three more valuable points, we improved our already healthy goal difference. Things were so very tight at the top that it had been suggested that the destiny of the League could well be settled on goal difference. That wasn't the way we wanted to win the Championship but, had it come down to that, you would not have heard us complaining too much.

"In that one game, Lee Chapman again demonstrated what a quality goalscorer he is. It is amazing that the man has so many critics because if his goal record is studied – not just at Leeds but throughout his long career – he has an amazing record of consistency. It just seems that no matter how well or badly Lee plays he will always get at least 20 goals per season. You really cannot ask for any more than that. Going to Highbury is rather like going to Anfield or Old Trafford in many respects because if you can take something away from the game you have to feel pleased with yourselves. We knew it was going to be very difficult for a wide variety of reasons. Their form had started to pick up, they had a lot to prove as the defending League Champions and the game was given that extra edge by being shown live on television. After Manchester United's rather surprising failure to defeat Wimbledon the previous day, it was a very good point for us and we were all in good heart on the journey back to Yorkshire."

Seven games left to play and Leeds were still desperately clinging to the top spot. With games in hand, Manchester United were still the clear favourites to lift the title for the first time in 25 years but their inability to seize the initiative was beginning to puzzle many people including, presumably, their manager, Alex Ferguson.

Surely, Leeds' next game was a formality. West Ham United, bottom of the First Division and seemingly doomed to return from whence they had come just 12 months earlier, at home. Three points, no question. The problem was that the Hammers had quite obviously not read a carefully prepared script. By refusing to take on the mantle of sacrificial lambs, West Ham gave Leeds the fright of their lives and further undermined the belief that the Championship was destined to come to rest at Elland Road. With Chris Whyte suspended and missing his first League game since his move from West Bromwich Albion back in 1990, the Leeds defence lacked its normal composure and was almost punctured on several occasions by West Ham forwards who used pace as a substitute for skill. Leeds swept towards their opponents' goalmouth in great numbers in the dying minutes in a frantic bid to steal victory but it was not to be and two crucial points were lost.

Top of the First Division at the end of March:

1. Manchester United   P 35   W 19   D 13   L 3   Pts 70
2. Leeds United   P 36   W 18   D 15   L 3   Pts 69

Gary McAllister comments: "To say the game ended goalless, I thought that was a real stormer of a match, I really did. Obviously, because West Ham were rooted to the bottom of the table, most people assumed that we would walk away with the points. I think they also thought we would run up a cricket score in the process.

"The problem was that they had not been officially relegated. Mathematically, at least, they could still survive if other results went their way. They were clutching at straws but they showed tremendous determination against us and I, for one, wouldn't begrudge them their point.

"Had their goalkeeper, Ludo Miklosko, not performed heroically, we probably would have won with some ease but he had a marvellous game; we just couldn't get the ball past him.

"We were disappointed but there was no point in being really downhearted. The race for the title had fluctuated so often – had changed direction so often – that we still believed that anything at all was possible. It was around this time that people started to question whether or not ourselves and Manchester United actually wanted to win the Championship. It was also around this time that Sheffield Wednesday started to move up the table and into contention. To be honest, we were never really worried about Wednesday because I think we all felt they had left it just a little too late. Had their challenge started a couple of weeks earlier – or had the season been a fortnight longer – who knows what might have happened? After all the talk of the two Uniteds, the title could have ended up at Hillsborough."

Leeds couldn't beat West Ham but their manager was to fare a good deal better when he was called before a Football Association disciplinary committee to explain remarks he had allegedly made to a linesman during the emphatic victory over Sheffield Wednesday at Hillsborough on 12 January. Wilkinson had always denied the charge which had been levelled at him. He had insisted that his comments were directed, not at the official but at one of his own players. As the Chairman of the newly formed Managers' Association it was important that he was cleared.

Although no one before had ever successfully defended himself against such a charge, Wilkinson was totally exonerated after using video evidence to back up his claim of innocence.

Gary McAllister, whose growing reputation was underlined by his inclusion in the Professional Footballers Association's composite First Division team, spent much of the month denying that he was shortly to leave Leeds and join Glasgow Rangers in a £3 million deal. "All I am looking to do is win a League Championship medal here. I am very happy at Elland Road," he said in an attempt to end the mounting speculation.

Although his squad was relatively small in comparison with that of Manchester United, Wilkinson allowed five players, including Imre Veradi, John McClelland and Bobby Davison, to join other clubs on loan. The transfer deadline passed quietly at Elland Road, the only arrival being Ali Mauchlen who signed on loan from Leicester City. He was nothing more than another interested spectator as the title race neared its climax and he departed back to Filbert Street without making a single appearance for his "new" club.

Saturday, 4 April, was the day it all threatened to go horribly wrong for Wilkinson and his team. Because of an early kick-off, by the time the thoroughbreds of the horse-racing world were hurtling over the intimidating fences of the Grand National course at Aintree, the players of Leeds United were locked away in their dressing-room at Maine Road having already been unseated at football's equivalent of Beecher's Brook.

The final scoreline of Manchester City 4 Leeds United 0 had been flashed around the country and in the eyes of so many the great Championship battle was finally at an end. It wasn't official, of course, far from it, but Leeds' heaviest defeat of the season prompted the nation's bookmakers to stop taking bets on the outcome. Manchester United were installed as the 6–1 on favourites with Leeds demoted to rank outsiders. Although few who were in attendance on that day would argue against the notion that City's margin of victory was flattering in the extreme, the players and management of Leeds United could find no solace in the fact that much of their football had been both fluent and attractive. There was not even dignity in despair, for the looks on the faces of the despondent Leeds team told its own worrying story.

Even Wilkinson, the ultimate optimist, found it difficult to maintain his normal level of enthusiasm. When he emerged from a near-silent dressing-room, the inevitable first question was; "Has the title now gone?" No doubt conscious that a defiant statement of intent would have carried little conviction under the circumstances he replied: "I don't know. What I do know is that we have now left ourselves with a great deal to do. If we can win our remaining five League games it could still be interesting. Having said that, the whole thing is now obviously out of our hands. We must now rely on Manchester United dropping points."

As the assembled media headed back to their telephones trying to decide whether or not Wilkinson had actually conceded the title, Gordon Strachan emerged and was asked the same question. "I don't know but I wouldn't put my mortgage on us winning the title now," he replied.

Gary McAllister recalls: "That was a really dreadful day. Although Manchester City thoroughly deserved to win the game, I don't honestly believe that they were four goals better than we were. We actually played some very good football, particularly when we were going forward. The only problem was that we couldn't score whereas they could. We didn't defend at all well on that afternoon.

"We are not mugs at Leeds United and as we sat in the dressing-room afterwards the general feeling was that the Championship had finally slipped away. You have to try and be as realistic as you can in this game and with just five games left to play – and with Manchester United ahead of us and with games in hand – we knew that we were definitely struggling. The problem was that while Manchester United were not playing as well as they had been earlier in the season, they were still picking up points.

"We fully appreciated that if they continued to do that, there was nothing at all we could do to stop them taking the title. It is so frustrating when your destiny is not in your own hands. Sitting around and waiting for other teams to drop points can be agonising. You try and concentrate on your own games and on your own performances but it can be very difficult.

"The only thing that gave us hope was the knowledge that Manchester United had a very heavy programme of four games in six days coming up. We all knew that they would struggle to win all those games so we felt there was still a glimmer of a chance.

"Mind you, to stay in contention at all we knew that we had to win most of our remaining games. The Easter period was going to be crucial. We set ourselves a target of collecting seven points from our next three fixtures against Chelsea, Liverpool and Coventry City. It was a difficult target but one which we managed to achieve. If we hadn't, the title would almost certainly have gone."

With Manchester United inactive because of their involvement in the Rumbelows Cup Final at Wembley hours later, Leeds entered the game against Chelsea at

Elland Road on 11 April requiring victory to return to the top of the table. Having seen their season effectively ended three weeks earlier when they were surprisingly despatched from the FA Cup by Sunderland in a quarter-final replay at Roker Park, Chelsea were playing for little more than pride.

Although it took some time to end the Londoners' stubborn resistance, victory was assured in the game's last quarter when Eric Cantona scored a stunning and majestic goal of immense quality. With four games left to go, Leeds edged a point ahead of their nearest rivals but they had now played two games more,

Top of the First Division on 11 April:

| 1. Leeds United | P 38 | W 19 | D 15 | L 4 | Pts 72 |
| 2. Manchester United | P 36 | W 19 | D 14 | L 3 | Pts 71 |

Gary McAllister reflects: "I suppose that the game against Chelsea will always be rememberd for Eric's astonishing goal. Although he tried to give the impression that he did that sort of thing all the time, he knew himself it was a very special moment.

"In that one moment, Eric proved to everybody what a skilful footballer he is. You won't see many better strikes than that one. It was a privilege to be on the pitch when it went in.

"The other significant thing about the afternoon was Lee Chapman's goal. It was his 20th of the season, which was a tremendous achievement bearing in mind that he had spent so long out of the side because of injury. It was good to be back on top again but we were still reliant upon Manchester United dropping points. All we could do was to keep the pressure on them by winning our games."

On Thursday, 16 April, Manchester United began the six-day programme which was eventually to decide the outcome of the League Championship. The first of four crucial League games in just 144 hours was against Southampton at Old Trafford.

Earlier in the season Southampton had curtailed United's interest in the FA Cup by winning a penalty shoot-out at the same venue. Once again, they were to produce a convincing performance which embraced character and spirit. Although their uncommon sense of adventure did, at one point, threaten to reap a handsome reward, the game was decided midway through the second half when Andrei Kanchelskis volleyed home in spectacular fashion. Manchester United were back in pole position despite a largely indifferent display.

Top of the First Division on 16 April:

1. Manchester United	P 37	W 20	D 14	L 3	Pts 74
2. Leeds United	P 38	W 19	D 15	L 4	Pts 72

There is undoubtedly a great deal of truth to the old adage which suggests that no team can consider themselves to be worthy champions of England unless they have proven their worth against Liverpool. Despite a season of rank inconsistency and debilitating injury problems, the Merseysiders were still a force to be reckoned with – especially at Anfield. Having defeated Graeme Souness's team at Elland Road seven months earlier, Leeds were pursuing an improbable League double over the eventual FA Cup winners.

With their chances of winning the title hanging by the slenderest of threads, it was naturally assumed that Leeds would cast a measure of caution to the wind and push relentlessly forward in search of three points. They didn't.

Only as the game entered its final 15 minutes did Leeds begin to lay siege to Bruce Grobbelaar's goal. Chances were created but squandered and the game ended in a goalless draw.

Although Manchester United had only picked up a point from a 1-1 draw against soon-to-be-relegated Luton Town at Kenilworth Road, it was suggested that Leeds, by refusing to gamble on all-out attack, had further lessened their chances of success. Howard Wilkinson was swift to disagree as he placed into clear perspective the challenge which is always proferred by Liverpool.

"I don't care what anybody says, this is a very good result for us. If you can come to a place like Anfield and get a point then I believe that you have done a good job. I am pleased with this result," he said. The intense rivalry between Merseyside and Manchester is such that, throughout the game, thousands of Liverpool supporters urged Leeds forward, almost wishing them to score against their own team.

Top of the First Division on 18 April:

1. Manchester United	P 38	W 20	D 15	L 3	Pts 75
2. Leeds United	P 39	W 19	D 16	L 4	Pts 73

Gary McAllister recalls: "I was a little surprised at the criticism which we received after the game at Liverpool. Just because we could have done with a victory, people – or, rather, the media – seemed to assume that we would change our attitude completely and rush about in a desperate bid to win the game.

"That is something which you just can't do at a place like Anfield. If you chase the game you are playing straight into their hands and they will punish you. Liverpool may have had a disappointing season by their own remarkably high standards but they still have so many good players and good players, when performing at home, will never allow the visiting team to dictate things.

"Liverpool is a big-time club with big-time players and they like nothing better than to play against – and beat – other big-time clubs. It is as simple as that. We were aware that they had a point to prove to their own supporters; they wanted to show that while they had struggled a wee bit, they were already getting ready for the following season. On top of that, they had won their way through to the FA Cup final, so several of those players who faced us were fighting for places at Wembley. They were all trying to catch the eye of Ronnie Moran.

"At the end of the day, we could have nicked that game because we saw a couple of our shots kicked off the line. On the other hand, Liverpool could say that *they* were somewhat unlucky because John Lukic had a wonderful game and made three or four world-class saves.

"I was fully aware that most of the Liverpool fans wanted us, and not Manchester United, to win the Championship. A few weeks earlier I had gone to Anfield to watch the UEFA Cup tie against Genoa and once people found out who I was, I was treated like royalty. I got the distinct impression that they were praying we could win the title."

The whole emphasis and balance of the League Championship was to change on Easter Monday – the day when it became glaringly apparent that Manchester United's mounting anxiety was on the verge of manifesting itself in total collapse and surrender.

Because it was highly probable that Leeds' game against Coventry City at Elland Road would have a significant impact on both the top and the bottom of the First Division, the kick-off had been delayed until early evening to accommodate yet another live television broadcast. Although it had seemed unlikely earlier in the day, by the time Gordon Strachan led his team out into the dying embers of a warm, spring afternoon, the dream of Championship glory had moved a step closer to becoming harsh reality.

Earlier, in front of an enormous and frenzied crowd at Old Trafford, Manchester United had sought to extend their lead at the top at the expense of Nottingham Forest, the team they had beaten just eight days earlier in the final of the Rumbelows Cup. With Forest unable to improve on a position of mid-table anonymity, it was, as they say, a home banker. With the scoreline blank, and with a little over eight minutes remaining, United were to pay a very high price for pouring forward in numbers as they searched for a decisive goal. Forest, the masters of the counter-attack, broke swiftly and at the end of the afternoon's one move of any real consequence, Scott Gemmill drilled home a low drive to give the visitors both victory and sweet revenge.

The news of United's defeat filtered through on to the Elland Road terracing shortly before the two teams emerged from their dressing-rooms. The air was heavy with expectancy. It was carnival time. Howard Wilkinson was later to confirm that his players were aware of their closest rivals' surprise defeat which quite possibly explains why it was Leeds struggled to overcome a side which was only narrowly to avoid relegation.

In the end Leeds were indebted to a rare, but priceless, goal by Chris Fairclough and a controversial Gary McAllister penalty. For once, the result was far more important than the performance. With less than a fortnight of the season left, Leeds United were at the top of the First Division, a point clear of a Manchester United side which still had a game in hand.

Top of the First Division on 20 April:

1. Leeds United	P 40	W 20	D 16	L 4	Pts 76
2. Manchester United	P 39	W 20	D 15	L 4	Pts 75

Gary McAllister remembers the day well: "It was inevitable that we would learn of the Manchester United result before we ran out on to the pitch because you can't hope to keep something that important away from the players. Even if we had been shielded from the news, we would have realised what had happened once we stepped out of the tunnel because the whole ground was in uproar. The result from Old Trafford had obviously been broadcast over the public address system and our fans were delirious. You would have thought we had already won the title, so strong was their reaction. Because Coventry City were also in desperate need of points, albeit for totally different reasons, we knew they were not going to lie down and let us stroll to victory. We were anticipating a very tough afternoon and we got one.

"I thought they approached the game very well, which can't have been all that easy bearing in mind the atmosphere. It took us a little while to get going but once we had found our rhythm I thought we played some very attractive football. All we needed was a breakthrough – a goal – to settle us down. It finally came from a rather unexpected source when big Chris Fairclough found himself with enough space and time to head over Steve Ogrizovic.

"We needed a second goal because Coventry looked quite useful on the counter-attack. When it came it was a curious one because Lloyd McGrath was adjudged to have handled a shot on the line. Maybe he did but to send him off was a little on the harsh side. Anyway, I was the happiest man in Elland Road when my penalty hit the back of the net.

"We were back on top but there was no great mood of celebration because we knew that if Manchester United were to win their last three games, they would be Champions and not us. It was still out of our hands. All we could do was hope that West Ham United would do us a favour two days later."

The favour which McAllister and his team-mates had demanded – but which they could scarcely have been anticipating – duly materialised at Upton Park on 22 April when Manchester United tasted defeat in a League game for only the fifth time all season, losing 1–0.

With a matter of only days to go, and for the first time in many months, Leeds' destiny was back in their own hands. After an absence of 18 years, the League Championship would be returned to Elland Road if Wilkinson's side could win their two remaining games against Sheffield United at Bramall Lane and Norwich City at home.

Top of the First Division on 22 April:

1. Leeds United	P 40	W 20	D 16	L 4	Pts 76
2. Manchester United	P 40	W 20	D 15	L 5	Pts 75
3. Sheffield Wednesday	P 40	W 21	D 10	L 9	Pts 73
4. Arsenal	P 40	W 13	D 14	L 8	Pts 68

Gary McAllister says: "I don't know whether or not I expected West Ham to beat Manchester United. Although West Ham were at the bottom of the table and facing certain relegation I knew they would put up a real fight if only to please what was a sell-out crowd.

"On the night that game was played, I was at a fund-raising function as part of Jim Beglin's testimonial appeal. It was a Karaoke evening at a Leeds social club. When it was announced that United had been beaten the whole place exploded. It was a remarkable sight. I found it very hard to believe at first but eventually it all began to sink in.

"It was finally in our hands; we were in the driving seat when it really mattered the most. It was a wonderful feeling to sit there in the midst of all those happy supporters and think that if we could win our last two games we would be the Champions of England. I really did fancy us to do it."

Sunday, 26 April, is a day which, in truth, many supporters of Leeds United thought would never come again – the day when their club was to be crowned as English Champions. It was a bizarre day, an unforgettable day of unparalleled drama, a day of triumph and a day when the eyes of even the toughest supporter were moistened by tears of joy.

Although the two great rivals still had two fixtures each left to fulfil, the outcome would be decided *if* Leeds defeated Sheffield United and *if* Manchester United were beaten by Liverpool at Anfield. Any other combination of results would leave the Championship unresolved until the season's final day.

With their game kicking off at noon, Leeds held an advantage even before a pass had been delivered. Three points at Bramall Lane would so reduce Manchester United's options that they would have to defeat Liverpool to maintain even a fleeting interest in the title.

Having risen into the top half of the table on a positive tidal wave of self-belief and renewed optimism, Sheffield United lay in wait for their Yorkshire rivals – confident, almost arrogant.

With so much at stake, the game was a scrappy and untidy affair, littered with free kicks and awash with elementary mistakes. Leeds appeared to have weathered a ferocious early storm but they fell behind in the 28th minute when veteran striker Alan Cork collected a fortuitous rebound before stabbing the ball beyond the unprotected John Lukic. The interval beckoned when Leeds drew level with a goal of comic proportions, Wallace turning the ball over the line with his knee after Gary Speed had hooked a clearance back into the penalty area.

Nineteen minutes after the re-start Leeds were in front when Jon Newsome arrived unannounced at the far post to head in Gary McAllister's superbly flighted free kick. That lead was to last for just four minutes. In the 68th minute Lee Chapman attempted to clear John Pemberton's low drive only to deflect the ball into his own net. As the game ebbed and flowed towards its conclusion, it seemed likely that Leeds would settle for a draw against the First Division's most improved side.

However, as the cities of Leeds and Manchester held their breath, there was one final twist to the plot; a sting in the tail. As Brian Gayle attempted to shepherd a harmless-looking pass back to his goalkeeper, Eric Cantona and Rod Wallace began to converge. In one moment of mind-numbing madness, Gayle headed the ball over Mel Rees and into the back of his own net.

The final whistle, 13 minutes later, precipitated scenes of joyous celebration both on and off the pitch. Leeds, for so long the underdogs, were almost home and dry. Victory over Norwich City would clinch the title if – and it was a big if – Manchester United could keep alive their hopes by putting Liverpool to the sword. If Alex Ferguson's side were found wanting at Anfield it was all over – official.

As the Leeds players began to drift homewards, Liverpool ruthlessly set about destroying a dream.

Ian Rush's first-ever goal against Manchester United would have been enough but as if to rub salt into a gaping wound, Liverpool scored again at the death through Mark Walters. As the Kop began to taunt the stunned Manchester United supporters by screaming "You will never win the title", West Yorkshire rose up as one man to acclaim a historic and magnificent triumph.

The wilderness years were finally at an end. The ghost of Don Revie had finally been exorcised. The party was about to begin.

Top of the First Division on 26 April:

1. Leeds United	P 41	W 21	D 16	L 4	Pts 79
2. Manchester United	P 41	W 20	D 15	L 6	Pts 75
3. Sheffield Wednesday	P 41	W 21	D 11	L 9	Pts 74

Gary McAllister savours the memory: "Even though Sheffield United were the form team, we still fancied our chances of going to Bramall Lane and getting a victory. With the Championship now clearly in sight, we were hyped up and just couldn't wait to get started.

"It was one of the craziest games I have ever played in. Some of the things that happened during the course of the 90 minutes were just bizarre. I don't think there was a really good goal scored all afternoon. It was like a pantomime out there.

"Despite the obvious pressures, I really enjoyed playing in the game because the atmosphere was absolutely superb in the ground. It was like a cup-tie with tackles flying about and mistakes being made by even the best of players.

"It wasn't a pretty game but I shall never, ever forget that afternoon for as long as I live. It was such an emotional occasion both for the players of Leeds United and for those wonderful supporters.

"I have to say that when the final whistle sounded, I was convinced that we had won the title. No disrespect to Manchester United but I did think that Liverpool would beat them.

"I watched the Anfield game on television but even when Liverpool scored that second and decisive goal, I wasn't leaping around or anything like that. To be honest, I began to really feel for the Manchester United players. I couldn't help but put myself in their place. I knew exactly how they must have felt as they saw the Championship slowly slipping away from their grasp. They will have been absolutely gutted.

"It took a little time for it all to sink in but, when it did, I was so very happy – not just for myself and for the other lads in the team but for everyone at the club and for all the fans. I had only been a part of Leeds United for a relatively short period of time and I was ecstatic so I knew how those people who have been around for years and years must have been feeling at that moment.

"As soon as we were confirmed as the new Football League Champions, it was a case of ringing around the lads and rallying the troops. Most of the players headed for a restaurant. It was party-time and, believe me, we had a brilliant evening.

"The thing about modern football is that you can't sit back for too long and bask in the glory; you have to start looking to the future almost immediately.

"We are now the Champions but that means we will have an even more difficult time next season. We will be there to be shot at. Everyone will want to try and knock us down. The pressure really starts here. I am sure that Arsenal will look back on this season and have many regrets about the way their defence of the title went. We must try and make sure that we are ready come August and that we do everything in our power to hang on to our crown.

"The other bonus is a place in the European Cup. I can't wait until we have a really big European team here at Elland Road. That is such an exciting prospect for me as a player.

"I think the future looks good. I am sure that the manager won't stand still; I am sure that he will be looking to bring in more new players which means that none of us can rest on our laurels.

"Things have happened so quickly for Leeds United that it is sometimes very difficult to take it all in. Three and a half years ago, the club was near the foot of the Second Division – now they are Champions. One of the reasons I signed for Leeds in the first place was I believed there was genuine potential here and I have been proved right. I can't praise our manager highly enough because all along he kept everything nice and low-key. He never once showed signs of panic and he always did his best to deflect any pressure away from the dressing-room. He handled everything superbly.

"We are all looking to the future with great optimism. Leeds United was a sleeping giant but that giant has woken up."

Just before 2.30 pm on 2 May, Gordon Strachan emerged from the bosom of his team-mates to collect the Barclay's League trophy and so confirm Leeds United's position as best team in English football.

Quite possibly the very last thing players who had spent the previous few days celebrating a great triumph wished to do was play football but, as Manchester United

101

did not need reminding, the season embraces 42 games. Guests of honour at a purely private party were Norwich City and while they did their utmost to put something of a dampener on the joyous proceedings they could not prevent Rod Wallace scoring a spectacular goal to give Leeds a victory which they fully deserved.

Over at Old Trafford, Alex Ferguson's fallen heroes belatedly found their scoring touch to defeat Tottenham Hotspur 3–1.

It was too little, too late. Leeds United had won the title by four clear points.

Final First Division Table, Season 1991–92:

1. Leeds United	P 42	W 22	D 16	L 4	Pts 82
2. Manchester United	P 42	W 21	D 15	L 6	Pts 78
3. Sheffield Wednesday	P 42	W 21	D 12	L 9	Pts 75

Chapter Nine

TALKING TITLES AND MAKING COMPARISONS

It must have been a little strange for the supporters of Leeds United to wake up on a summery morning in late April to be faced by the realisation that no longer did they require thick skins and long memories to follow their club. The "perhaps it was all a dream" scenario will have been prevalent in many a West Yorkshire household as the task of placing into clear perspective a famous triumph begun in earnest. One glance at the morning newspapers was sufficient to confirm that a long-held vision of seemingly preposterous dimensions was finally reality. Hans Christian Andersen, it would seem, was alive and well and sharing a flat with the Brothers Grimm in Bramley or Seacroft.

"Wilko's Wonders!" and "Champions!" screamed the banner headlines. Pictures of jubilant, almost disbelieving, Leeds players filled every available page. It was all true yet still slightly unbelievable. Predictably, the centre of attention was one, Howard Wilkinson, the weaver of fantasies; the man who had not only reared a fine goose but who had cajoled it into laying the golden egg.

With a degree of reluctance which was, perhaps, understandable, Wilkinson was centre-stage for the first time all season. Having stalked the shadows for so long he was ushered forward into the spotlight and urged to open his heart.

Amid the euphoric scenes of the previous day, Wilkinson, by all accounts, had been far more concerned with feeding his stomach than his imagination. Having

103

departed from Bramall Lane in a suitably contented mood, he had made the short journey home and sat down to a traditional Sunday lunch. Manchester United, he assured anyone who would listen, were not on the menu.

At the very moment his hour of triumph and destiny beckoned, Wilkinson was found to be a man very much at odds with himself. Although he craved the glory which was shortly to follow, he was able to divorce himself from proceedings to such an extent that his fertile mind turned not to matters of sport but to matters of compassion.

As he was to admit, between 3 pm and 4.45 pm on Sunday, 26 April, his thoughts were centred around a fellow professional, Alex Ferguson, as Manchester United locked horns with Liverpool at Anfield. "I did not watch the Liverpool game on television. I had a nice, relaxed Sunday lunch with those people who are nearest and dearest to me," he said. "I knew what was happening at Anfield because my five-year-old son, Ben, sneaked away from the dining-table to watch the match in his bedroom.

"I just couldn't sit down and watch it. If there was going to be an execution, I didn't want to see it. I didn't want to be a part of it. It had been a long season and I couldn't sit there and watch a man like Alex Ferguson suffer.

"Of course, when the final whistle went at Anfield and we were confirmed as the new League Champions I was both jubilant and emotional. Never in my wildest dreams did I imagine that we would be as successful as this. It was a case of 'stop the world I want to get off'. I really couldn't believe it had happened.

"It was the realisation of a dream and one of the most fantastic days of my life. When I was only 24 years old, I thought that I had better become a manager because, as a player, I was nothing more than a bricklayer's labourer. I decided a long time ago that my ambition was to win the First Division Championship and then the European Cup.

"Even I could not have envisaged when I took over at Elland Road and formulated my blueprint for the future that success like this would come so soon. When I arrived at the club in October 1988, we were second from bottom of Division Two and it looked an impossible dream," he added. It was after the season's final League fixture against Norwich City on 2 May that Wilkinson sought to fully explain his feelings and emotions. It had been a long and tiring week of celebration but Wilkinson was clearly in the mood to talk.

"This is the first time anything like this has happened to me. It has now sunk in but it is that old thing – anticipation is better than realisation. I think I have enjoyed getting here more than actually being here. My players have done a simply magnificent job – 82 points, 20 clean sheets, unbeaten at home in the League.

"Having won it for the first time, I would love to win it again and again but, in all honesty, nothing can be sweeter than this moment. You just can't follow this. The key all along has been performances and that will have to be the same next season. You must forget about winning and you must forget about losing. You must forget about cups and trophies, you must concentrate on the actual performances.

"While ever I am the manager at this club, if I think that my players have delivered the sort of performances which they are capable of then I will be a happy man. If those performances are not good enough to win games on that day or in that year then so be it – that is sport. Obviously, in football that sort of argument sometimes isn't good enough for the supporters but you have to learn to live with that.

"When we were still in contention at Christmas, I knew that we had a chance. I knew that we had to keep going because in the previous season we had been down the same road. We were not Championship contenders on that occasion but we had reached the semi-finals of two cup competitions and we were faced by a heavy programme of fixtures.

"Having faced a heavy schedule of four important games in just six days, I remembered how we felt at the time and I knew that Manchester United were going to be faced by the same problems. While we had to pick ourselves up, in a psychological sense, after our nearest rivals had knocked us out of the two major cup competitions, I knew all about the workload which they would be faced by and, whether you like it or not, the workload is a fact of life.

"If you are successful in this country you find yourselves doing overtime and sometimes you pay for overtime. I just kept telling my lads to keep going – keep going until somebody wins the race. My players nerved it out well and stood firm. When you consider that we started the season with what I considered to be the fourth-strongest squad in the Division, we have done magnificently well.

"We are not asking to be compared with anyone, past or present. We are only asking to be allowed to enjoy this success. I am not saying that we are better than any other team which has won it in the past and I am not saying that we are better than any team which will win it in the future.

"To be honest, whether we deserve credit or whether we actually receive credit doesn't really bother me. My players now have a League Championship-winners medal and you can't take that away from them. All we could do was win the title and we did just that.

"There are lots of games which stand out from the season. Away from home, I remember our performances at Sheffield Wednesday, Aston Villa and Chelsea. At home, we did very well against Manchester City at a time when they were in form. I thought one of our best displays, because we were up against a very good side, was against Manchester United in the FA Cup when we lost, 1–0. Liverpool at Anfield was a very, very important game. The players did exactly what I wanted them to do – they got a result.

"This is an opportunity for this club and for this city to go forward. Next season is a new season and what we have done this time will not make a blind bit of difference. Everyone will be out to beat us. We must try and improve and if that means bringing in new players then that is the way it will have to be," he added.

Although some sections of the national media and several so-called footballing experts sought to somehow undermine Leeds' achievement by suggesting that the First Division is, at present, second-rate, most people were fulsome in their praise.

Jimmy Armfield, who managed the club between 1974 and 1978, was one of the few to admit that he was not unduly surprised by Leeds' swift return to a position of prominence. "I have been very, very impressed by what I have seen at Leeds United over the past couple of seasons but I am not terribly surprised at this success," he said.

"Once the Leeds board had signalled its intent by making money available to its manager I always thought that they were in with a shout. The thing is, there has always been enormous potential at Elland Road. When you get right down to the bottom line, Leeds do deserve some reward for investing such a lot of hard cash.

"Having money is one thing, spending it well is another and I think Howard Wilkinson has done exceptionally well in terms of his dealings within the transfer market. Having built up a useful squad – one which took them back into the First Division – he brought in players of experience and quality.

"Several individuals have enjoyed really outstanding seasons – I am thinking of players like John Lukic, David Batty and Gary Speed. Defensively, the side is very sound indeed.

"Wilkinson was definitely the right kind of man to bring in after Billy Bremner had been dismissed. He was a manager with a good track record and a real background in football," he added.

Armfield believes that the Leeds board was right to abandon the unsuccessful policy of asking former players to return to the club as manager. "It was a bold decision but it was unquestionably the correct one," he says. "After trying three of Don Revie's old boys in Allan Clarke, Eddie Gray and Bremner, there was a need to break free from the old traditions. I think that everybody connected with the club felt that it was the right time for a change of direction: a change of emphasis.

"It is funny, you know, with a little more luck any one of those three men could have made it as a manager with

Leeds. Personally, I have always been of the opinion that if you have served a club well as a player you are tempting fate if you decide to retrace your steps. Thankfully, the Leeds public will not remember Clarke, Gray and Bremner as managerial failures but as great footballers. That is the way it should be.

"In many respects, Wilkinson picked just the right point to arrive at the club. Although they were struggling to stay afloat in the Second Division, they were ripe for success because the money was available. It was a totally different scenario to the one which I had faced after succeeding Brian Clough in 1974. When I took over I had a squad full of experienced, if aging, players but no money. Howard found himself with a squad full of inexperienced players but with plenty of money.

"I do not wish to take anything at all away from Leeds and what they have achieved but the simple fact of the matter is that, in football, you can do little or nothing unless you have the necessary financial clout. If you look at the successful clubs over the past five or ten years, the ones which have done well are the ones who have had money available to them.

"One man who does deserve very special praise is Leslié Silver, the Leeds chairman. He was not only the man who had his hands on the purse-strings but he was the man with the vision. He was the guiding light and he deserves to enjoy this success because without him Leeds would not be where they are today.

"Winning the first, big prize is the hardest thing to do so I wouldn't be at all surprised to see Leeds United consolidate this new-found position. They have done the hard bit, now they must try and do it again and again. It will not be easy but they have the team, they have the manager and they have the financial infrastructure.

"The whole thing is beginning to take off once again. Many thousands of Leeds supporters will be experiencing something new because they won't be able to recall the events of the Sixties and Seventies. Howard Wilkinson has managed to get the Leeds bandwagon rolling once again and I, for one, am absolutely delighted."

Terry Yorath, a member of the Championship-winning side of 1974, still regularly attends games at Elland

Road and has no doubts that Leeds are, indeed, worthy champions. "I am getting a little tired of hearing the suggestion that Leeds United only won the title because Manchester United saw fit to throw it away. It is beginning to sound like the players at Old Trafford deliberately gave it to Leeds out of an act of kindness," he says.

"Let's get one thing straight – Leeds are worthy Champions. They deserve to be recognised as the best team in the Football League. They probably won't be but I am sure that won't unduly bother Howard Wilkinson and his players. They have proved themselves to be the best and they should be given credit and respect.

"Am I surprised by the speed of this massive transformation? You bet I am. It really is remarkable what has been achieved in such a short space of time. Wilkinson has done a truly amazing job at the club and has proved himself to be, arguably, the best manager in the country.

"I suppose that it was inevitable that people would seek to make comparisons between the current Leeds team and the one I played in 18 years ago. I can't see the point, to be honest. It is today that matters and the Leeds team of today is the best.

"The Leeds team of the Seventies was a great one – there is no doubt at all about that. The thing is that the passing of time has served to embroider reputations and to change opinions. There is no point in being coy about it – the team I played in was almost universally hated. No one liked us, not the opposition, not the media, not the game's governing bodies.

"The thing was, we were so successful that everybody seemed to resent it. People say that we were too hard and too professional but they seem to forget that we had many players of outstanding ability. Now, 18 years on, people have started to look back at that team, and what it achieved, with affection. It is a crazy situation.

"The players of today are different as is the style of football. They are far more athletic than we were. If you see a video of football back in the Seventies it looks as though it is in slow motion. No, there is no point attempting to draw comparisons. It might be fun but it is also futile.

"I have enjoyed watching Wilkinson's team a great deal this season. They have some tremendously talented players – and several unsung heroes. Take someone like Chris Whyte for example. He had a brilliant season. He was solid, reliable and totally consistent yet when the short list for the Professional Footballers Association awards was published, which two defenders were included? Gary Pallister and Steve Bruce, that's who!

"Lee Chapman may score a lot of goals but he is still one of the most underrated and neglected players in the modern game. When people talk of great Leeds United forwards they mention the likes of Allan Clarke, Peter Lorimer and Mick Jones – but never Lee Chapman. They should, because his goals-per-game ratio is up there with the very best of them.

"Needless to say, I think the future looks really bright once again. I think I can say with some confidence that Leeds United is in very safe hands. I think that Howard will be quite content to stay at the club for the next five years or so and if things have gone well, he will probably look for something even bigger – quite possibly the England job.

"If he is offered the chance to take control of the England national side he will find himself under real pressure. He would have to sit down and think about what has happened to England managers in the past. In the end, I suppose, it all comes down to the quality of your working life," he added.

Paying glowing tributes to another club is never easy for rival managers but, on this occasion at least, many were willing to remove the blinkers and salute the revival of a famous club.

Joe Royle of Oldham Athletic was effusive: "Heartiest congratulations are in order because Leeds United and Howard Wilkinson have done a truly remarkable job over the past few years.

"I think it is good for football that someone has broken the stranglehold which Liverpool and Arsenal seemed to have established on the First Division. Variety, as they say, is the spice of life and I think it is in everyone's best interests that the game's major honours are shared around. If the same couple of clubs win everything year after year, the supporters will start to get a little disillusioned, which is perfectly understandable.

"What Leeds United have achieved in the space of three and a half years will give hope to every club outside of the First Division. They have shown exactly what can happen if a club is run properly from top to bottom, from board-room to dressing-room.

"I suppose, in a way, they did have something of a head start because as a club Leeds United have always had the resources, the support and the tradition.

"The detractors will, of course, say that Manchester United blew it but no one gave Leeds United the title. They had to fight and scrap for it right to the bitter end. It was won over nine months not over Easter when Manchester United's form started to slip away.

"The First Division is the hardest league in the world to win so Leeds have every reason to feel proud of themselves. Howard Wilkinson has proved himself to be a manager with great flair: one who plans and organises things exceptionally well.

"Having won the title, Leeds now face a very testing time. As top dogs everyone will be lining up to take a pop at them. They will do well to retain the Championship because very few sides have managed that in recent years.

"I have been impressed by them. They have some very talented footballers. If you are looking for the key man, Wilkinson apart, you need look no further than Gordon Strachan."

Ron Atkinson of Aston Villa was equally complimentary: "Leeds have a set pattern of play, one which is very difficult to combat. They play very well as a team but the added bonus is that they have players of individual excellence.

"I know that people have been saying that my old club, Manchester United, threw the Championship away but you have to give credit to Leeds for sticking at it. They kept plugging away in determined manner even when all looked lost.

"The thing which did impress me was how much character they showed after suffering a bad result. They didn't lose that often but when they did there was never any hangover, they always seemed to bounce straight back and that is a great quality to have. Much of the credit must go to Howard Wilkinson because he handled the pressure very well indeed. Naturally, I was impressed when they defeated us 4–1 at Villa Park; they played really, really well. Having said that, we should have beaten them in the return fixture at Elland Road. We had a Dalian Atkinson goal disallowed during that match and I still can't work out why that was. Anyway, full marks to them. I am particularly pleased for Gordon Strachan for obvious reasons. He is a marvellous player and his signing was absolutely crucial to Leeds' rapid development.

"As for next season and the extra challenge of the European Cup, I don't really know how they will fare. They are a good team but they still do not have that many players of experience.

"It might be unfashionable to say it but I think it is good that English football has a strong Leeds United side again. To be honest, they weren't actually that bad a team under the managership of Billy Bremner."

Trevor Francis of Sheffield Wednesday rates Leeds United: "I was very impressed by the way Leeds played throughout the season. I liked their style and their approach to the game.

"To be perfectly honest, I did not think they would win the League Championship this season but I don't suppose I am alone in saying that. I think it's fair to say that they have surprised everyone – possibly even themselves.

"Howard Wilkinson has not only given them a nice blend of youth and experience, he has given them a choice of options in terms of strategical approach. If they are up against a good, genuine footballing team they can compete on equal terms but they can also be aggressive and direct when the occasion demands.

"Although full credit must go to them for the way they stuck at it, I have to say that I believe Manchester United really did throw away the Championship this season. I know that people turn around at the end of each and every season and say someone threw something away but this time I do believe it is true. With only a few weeks to go, Alex Ferguson's team was ahead and had games in hand and you really can't ask for any more than that. They must be terribly disappointed over at Old Trafford – I bet they are still coming to terms with the fact that they are not the Champions.

"One of the problems with football in this country is that there are so many different competitions to enter that you end up paying a very high price if you are successful. Good sides have been losing out on major honours because of this for many years now.

"I do still believe that the best team in English football at the moment is Arsenal although they do say that the final First Division table never lies. Many people said that had George Graham's team started their impressive run a couple of weeks earlier – or had the season been a fortnight longer – they would have possibly retained the title. I don't believe that – I think that if the season had gone on for just a little bit longer my side may have sneaked up on the rails and taken it!

"Howard has done a quite remarkable job since he moved to Elland Road from Hillsborough but that doesn't really surprise me all that much. I know him quite well and he is one of the most dedicated and thorough managers in the game. Even so, I think Leeds have surpassed even their own expectations with this success.

"The fact that everything at Manchester United seemed to be geared to winning the title for the first time in 25 years probably helped Leeds. Manchester United expected to win it this time, whereas I don't think Leeds did. Consequently, the pressure at Elland Road was nothing like as severe as it was at Old Trafford. I saw Manchester United play at Old Trafford quite a lot after the turn of the year and I suspected they might end up dropping crucial points if only because of the dreadful state of their playing surface.

"Next season? A lot will depend on whom Howard signs during the summer months. His signings last year – Rod Wallace, Tony Dorigo and Steve Hodge – helped to improve things, so I am sure he will be looking to do it again."

Peter Reid of Manchester City comments: "I have always liked Leeds United as a club so I am happy to see them back at the top of the game. Throughout my career I have always relished playing at Elland Road because, irrespective of how the team was doing, the support was always marvellous.

"Yes, they do deserve to be League Champions because they won more games than anybody else and lost fewer games than anybody else. That's it in a nutshell, really. Ever since I became a professional footballer, the people within the game whom I have really admired – Howard Kendall and Bob Paisley for example – have always insisted that the best team always wins the title. Who am I to disagree with a sentiment like that? The key thing was their sense of purpose and their refusal to quit. After we had beaten them, 4–0, at Maine Road, even I thought that, perhaps, their big chance had finally gone. It is to their eternal credit that they kept on going when a lesser side would have folded. Their spirit was probably the deciding factor in the final count because, in terms of quality, there wasn't a great deal between them and Manchester United. I thought our neighbours were going to win it but I wasn't all that surprised when they started to drop points near the end.

"Like everybody else within football, I am full of admiration for what Howard Wilkinson has achieved at Leeds. He took a club which was going nowhere in particular and dragged it screaming into the Nineties. The present Leeds team reminds me a little of the Everton side I played in in the mid–Eighties, in so much as it is very much a side without stars. Their success has been built upon good, solid team-work. They have a very good goalkeeper, a reliable and mobile back four and a very impressive and productive midfield quartet. David Batty is a terrific little player, Gary Speed is a diamond, Gary McAllister is very classy and there isn't too much you can say about Gordon Strachan that hasn't been said a million times.

"Up front they have three players – Lee Chapman, Rod Wallace and Eric Cantona – who always look likely to score. It is a very good, well-balanced team."

Dave Bassett of Sheffield United says: "I know Howard Wilkinson quite well, which explains why I am not surprised at the speed of this transformation.

"He is a very private person, someone who doesn't worry too much about what other managers say or about what is written about him and his team in the newspapers. I think that people have underestimated him in the past.

"Leeds United are very worthy Champions in my opinion. It is alright people turning around, after the event, and saying that Arsenal or Sheffield Wednesday could have won the title if the season had been a little longer but the simple fact is that you have to do it, consistently, over a whole season – not just the last few months. I think that they should be able to sustain their new-found momentum because they enjoy such a massive support, and with that comes money. Even if they do not successfully defend their title it certainly won't be the end of the world."

Terry Venables of Tottenham Hotspur says: "It is just like a fairy-tale, isn't it? The thing is there isn't normally room for fairy-tales in this game of ours. During their first season back in the top flight they knocked us all giddy with their football and now they are League Champions. Howard Wilkinson has done a magnificent job – the only problem now is repeating this success next season."

Alan Hansen, a former Liverpool and Scotland international defender, is delighted: "I am genuinely pleased for Leeds United because they provided me with some wonderful entertainment throughout the course of the season.

"Like everybody else, I thought the League Championship was on its way to Old Trafford. They were in such a strong position towards the end that I just couldn't see any way they could throw it away. They did, though.

"Although Howard Wilkinson's side has proved itself to be capable of playing football of the very highest order, I was surprised they finished on top because after Christmas they seemed to lose their way. For a while, they tended to throw everyone and everything forward. It seemed to be a last, desperate toss of the dice. I just couldn't see a team which appeared to have thrown all caution to the wind winning the biggest prize in English football. Strangely, they calmed down as the pressure began to build up on them. Whether this was the manager's influence breaking through to the surface or whether it was because they thought they had blown it, I just don't know.

"I had written them off after the mauling they received at Maine Road but they displayed remarkable character in the weeks after that defeat. They never once gave the impression that they felt they were pursuing a lost cause; they simply kept their heads down and dug in. In the end the fact that Leeds were not going to be shaken off definitely told on Manchester United. They seemed to panic at the crucial stage. Once that had happened it was all over.

"Before Christmas they played some delightful football and even after the turn of the year they continued to underline their confidence with performances like the one against Sheffield Wednesday at Hillsborough. Of all the teams I saw in action last season, they were without a doubt the most exciting. They have started to play the game in a way which I like and admire very much. The days when Leeds United were known as a dour, unattractive team have most definitely now gone.

"In Wilkinson they have a very, very astute leader. When I saw them play out a goalless draw against Liverpool at Anfield as the campaign began to near its climax, I initially felt a little disappointed that they hadn't tried harder to force a victory. It was only afterwards that I realised that Wilkinson was correct when he said he viewed it as a good performance and a valuable point. I realised that if I had been playing for Leeds United on that day, I too would have been pleased with a draw.

"No one can deny them the right to be the Champions because they displayed a resilience and a level of consistency which no other side was capable of matching. I think they learned so much from the previous season when they were in contention until blowing up around February. That is experience and it will grow with each and every passing season.

"People have already started saying that it was hardly a vintage year in the First Division but try telling that to the players and supporters of the Football League Champions!

"Their success was built upon a defence which, in my opinion, has been overlooked, neglected and underestimated. Chris Whyte and Chris Fairclough established a terrific partnership in the middle and the two full-backs, Mel Sterland and Tony Dorigo, were excellent.

"Their strength in the middle of the park is well known. All four men are quality players and they have a lovely blend of aggression and subtlety. Add to all that Lee Chapman and Rod Wallace and you have a very talented side.

"Over the next couple of years they will be looking to win the title at least once more and they will be striving to achieve consistency and continuity. It won't be easy but I think they could be a major force for some time to come."

Alex Ferguson of Manchester United is generous in defeat: "Leeds United won the title because they made fewer mistakes than any other side in the First Division – it really is as simple as that.

"Anybody who talks about this being an ordinary League is talking rubbish because it is still as difficult to win as it ever was. Losing out has had a numbing effect on us and I don't know how we will get over it but we will find a way.

"I am still very proud of my team. People like Bryan Robson and Brian McClair show what we are all about. You can't leave your character behind in the dressing-room and what you see on the pitch is a true reflection of them as human beings.

"Of course, this is a big disappointment but looking back it was not a bad season. We won the Rumbelows Cup and the European Super Cup and we had thousands of people coming in through the turnstiles to enjoy it. We are good enough and we are young enough to have another go at the League next time.

"This has been a marvellous achievement by Leeds United and no one can take that away from them."

Although the success of the modern Leeds United will inevitably push even further into history the achievements of Don Revie's famous side of the Seventies, the players of a long-gone, but not forgotten, era were similarly anxious to express their delight.

Norman Hunter comments: "I really do believe that the late Don Revie would have taken great pleasure from watching this Leeds United team. Obviously, I have been asked, on several occasions, to draw some sort of comparison between this side and the one of 1974.

"You can't really do that and I shall explain why. People, if they can, should try and make comparisons only between Howard Wilkinson's side and the Leeds side which won promotion from the Second Division at the end of the 1963-64 season. You just can't make a worthwhile comparison between the team of 1992 and the teams which won the League Championship in 1969 and 1974, because by the time those titles were won the team had been together for several years and was crammed full of top-quality internationals.

"This Leeds United side has actually done far better than we did; they have won the Championship much quicker than we did and that is a marvellous achievement.

"The game is so very different nowadays. It is far quicker, there is a lot more tackling, there are more offsides, more goals from set-pieces. What we are talking about are two quite different eras. It is rather like asking if Joe Louis would have beaten Mike Tyson – you really can't say because things have changed so very much.

"This success is wonderful for the club and for its loyal supporters. I think that they managed to get out of the Second Division a year ahead of schedule and I think they have also won the Championship ahead of schedule.

"I have said a few times that it is not always the best team which wins the title but it is the team which is most determined and which wants success the most. I do think that, overall, Manchester United had the better of the two squads and that in certain areas they had the better players. However, Leeds had the better sense of organisation and their spirit and will to win was that little bit stronger in the end.

"Manchester United's big strength was their defence – they didn't concede many goals at all but having said that, the Leeds defence, while not as good on paper, also performed superbly. If you have a good defence then you will always have a real chance of collecting the big honours.

"Three weeks before the end of the season, I thought the title was most definitely on its way to Old Trafford and I suspect quite a few of the Leeds players possibly did too. But I said all along that if Leeds were offered a second bite of the cherry – and if they accepted that invitation – they would get their noses back in front and hang on. They stuck to their task superbly.

"If one of the closing pack had got their act together a little bit earlier it would have been even more interesting because both Leeds and Manchester United were definitely starting to falter towards the end. Arsenal were my tip for the title before the start of the season but they were never to fully recover from a disastrous start to their League programme.

"Under Howard Wilkinson, Leeds United have now laid the foundation stones. I am sure that Howard will seek to bring in new players before the start of the new season; he will be looking to make his senior squad even stronger before the defence of the title begins.

"It is very difficult to pick out a couple of individual players and say that they were primarily responsible for the success. All good sides start at the back and in John Lukic Leeds have an outstanding goalkeeper who was superb for much of the season.

"Nobody should overlook the contribution made by Lee Chapman either. He is not everybody's cup of tea nor is he the most technically gifted of footballers but he hit the target 20 times again and Leeds would not have won the Championship without him."

Eddie Gray also sings the praises of the present Leeds United team: "To have achieved promotion and then this in such a short time is absolutely tremendous. They can go all the way now; there is no reason why they should not continue their success. As for Europe, well, you can never tell.

"I have got nothing but praise for Howard Wilkinson. This is a fantastic achievement."

Allan Clarke comments: "There is a lot to build on and I am sure Howard Wilkinson and the board are quite aware of the task that lies ahead and will not get carried away. It is not always the best team that wins the League but the most consistent and Leeds have certainly been that. There is still a lot of building to do but I am sure that under Howard's leadership the team, and the club, will go from strength to strength."

Billy Bremner declares: "I am delighted for Howard Wilkinson, the players and the supporters. They are the best fans in the world and they deserve this success as much as the players do. It is a proud day for the club and for the city.

"Players like David Batty and Gary Speed are still learning the game but they are the future of Leeds United and it must be great for them to have achieved something like this so early in their careers. It is good for the game that there is now a third force to contest the major honours with Liverpool and Arsenal."

Peter Lorimer seconds that emotion: "The supporters of Leeds United deserve this success such a lot because they have waited a very long time for something like this to happen.

"Nothing would give me greater pleasure than to see this team go on to win the European Cup and they couldn't have a better tactician than Howard Wilkinson to guide them towards that target.

"There has been a suspicion in some quarters that players from the Don Revie era somehow resent the success of the current Leeds team but that is rubbish.

"Howard has players who can adapt to any system which he demands and he has proved himself to be one of the most astute managers in the game. England needs a footballing brain like his to help restore our reputation in Europe. We have lost contact with the way the game is played on the Continent. It showed in Arsenal's match against Benfica – they could not cope with a team willing to run at them.

"Believe me, the foreign teams will not be looking forward to coming to Elland Road next season. The fanatical crowd will be worth a goal start."

Gary Speed heads goalwards during the game against Crystal Palace at Elland Road, 18 January 1992

Gary Speed takes a tumble but still causes panic in the Notts County defence during the League game at Elland Road, 1 February 1992

Goal! David Batty acknowledges the crowd's applause after scoring against Notts County, 2 February 1992

*Eric Cantona goes close to marking his debut with a goal against Oldham
Athletic at Boundary Park, 8 February 1992*

*Rising to the occasion . . . Gary Speed out jumps the Oldham Athletic defence
during the 2—0 defeat at Boundary Park, 8 February 1992*

Lee Chapman outjumps Kevin Richardson during the goalless draw against Aston Villa at Elland Road, 3 March 1992

Gary Speed and Rod Wallace combine to end an Aston Villa attack during the game at Elland Road, 3 March 1992

Hot Rod . . . Rod Wallace scores in the 3—1 victory over Tottenham Hotspur at White Hart Lane, 7 March 1992

Chris Whyte gets to grips with Arsenal's Alan Smith, 22 March 1992

Heading back to the top. Rod Wallace scores during the 3—0 win over Chelsea at Elland Road, 11 April 1992

Leeds search for a breakthrough in the crucial game against Coventry City at Elland Road, 20 April 1992

A rare goal by Chris Fairclough sets Leeds on the way to a crucial victory over Coventry City at Elland Road on Easter Monday, 22 April 1992

Jon Newsome swoops to head in Leeds' second goal in the dramatic 3—2 victory over Sheffield United at Bramall Lane. Three hours later, Leeds were confirmed as Football League Champions, 26 April 1992

Norwich City's John Polston reaches a Gordon Strachan cross just ahead of Tony Dorigo in the season's final match, 2 May 1992

Poetry in motion . . . Gary Speed displays the grace and balance which has endeared him to the Elland Road crowd

Chapter Ten

PATIENCE REWARDED: THE SUPPORTERS' VIEW

When Howard Wilkinson moved forward to clutch the microphone and address the many thousands who had assembled to pay tribute to their victorious team at the conclusion of an emotional drive through the city on 3 May, one of the first things he said was that he believed the supporters of Leeds United to be the "best in the country".

It was an opinion which was shared, and voiced, by a long succession of people connected with the club as the full magnitude and true significance of the event began to finally sink in.

While it is unquestionably true that all football supporters are members of a very special breed, irrespective of where their allegiance may lie, precious few can claim parity with the followers of Leeds United in terms of commitment and loyalty.

The dictionary definition of the word "fanatic" – whence the term "fan" derives – is: "A person whose enthusiasm or zeal for something is extreme or beyond normal limits." Precisely.

It hasn't always been easy supporting Leeds United. Those who were born after 1970 will find it exceedingly difficult to isolate many moments of genuine satisfaction. There have been very few moments to cherish, to savour, in recent years.

However, despite being force-fed an unattractive diet of broken promises, Leeds' support has resolutely stood firm, often adopting the Micawber-like attitude that something good would eventually turn up if they waited around for long enough.

Once reviled for behaviour which was both patently anti-social and totally unacceptable, Leeds supporters are now respected. At long last the visit of several thousand partisan Yorkshiremen need not strike fear into the hearts and minds of local residents and policemen alike. In many respects it is a case of mirror-imaging, for just as the Leeds United team has been transformed for the better in recent years, so has the Leeds United support. This is, perhaps, an even greater and more significant achievement. For the first time in 18 years Leeds supporters, quite literally, have something to shout about.

STEPHEN MILLS (aged 35, electrical wholesaler):
"When I was a youngster back in the late Fifties and early Sixties, Leeds was a city which really wasn't too concerned with football. It was a rugby league city. You either went to watch Leeds RL, Bramley or Hunslet, depending on where you lived or depending on who your father supported.

"It was very simple up until the mid-Sixties – rugby during the winter and cricket, at Headingley, during the summer. It really wasn't too difficult a choice to make because Leeds United were struggling in the Second Division and with no real pedigree or history to back them up – or to attract new fans, few people seemed to go.

"Of course, we still played football like everybody else. Football was always my first love and I would never dream of taking a rugby ball out on the park near where I was brought up in Stanningley.

"We all hoped that United would do well but too often it was a case of listening to the results come in at 4.40 pm on a Saturday evening and hearing of another defeat. They were going nowhere until Don Revie started to work his magic. Even during the 1963–64 season when it became clear that the club was going to win promotion from the Second Division, I didn't go along to Elland Road. That changed once they forced their way back into the big-time.

"As a school-kid it was relatively easy to get along to Elland Road and watch the club because they were desperately keen to "hook" a new army of supporters. From what I can remember, every school in the city was given two or three free passes which were handed out on a rotation basis to members of the school football team after games on a Saturday morning. I don't know whether this sort of scheme is still in operation today but I somehow doubt it. Football in the Nineties is certainly far more of a business than it ever was during the Sixties.

"This free ticket idea worked because within a matter of months I was going down to home matches irrespective of whether I got in for nothing or not; I just wanted to be there because things were starting to go well.

"It goes without saying that Revie's team was magnificent. They just seemed to spring up from nowhere, almost overnight. It was very difficult to believe that most of those famous names had, in fact, been at the club for a while – since they were youngsters.

"It was like being aboard an out-of-control roller-coaster during the Sixties and Seventies. It was a strange feeling because the team was so good, so efficient, that you went along to games – particularly the home games – completely confident that Leeds would win. I remember that it almost became boring at one point. It was simply a question of how large the margin of victory would be.

"When things are good you think it is never going to end; you think the success will go on forever. It doesn't, of course. Once Revie had foolishly decided to pack it in and take the England job, things started to go horribly wrong. In the wake of Revie's departure it turned into a long procession of managers who were either unlucky or just not good enough. Brian Clough, Jimmy Armfield, Jock Stein, Jimmy Adamson all came and went before the Leeds board seemed to climb aboard some sort of time-machine. Instead of looking forward, they began to look back.

"Things were going from bad to worse out on the field of play but all the board could think about was trying to revive the glory of the Revie era. As a result we ended up with Allan Clarke, Eddie Gray and Billy Bremner as team manager. Now, don't get me wrong, all three were wonderful, wonderful players but . . . managers? . . . no, I don't think so. Where are they now? Have they moved on from Leeds and done well? No, they haven't. Appointing them was a mistake – a very big mistake.

"It was only when it dawned on our board of directors that this Liverpool-style dressing-room to managerial office routine wasn't working that we started to get things right. Once Bremner had been sacked in 1988, I wanted Howard Kendall as our manager. I just thought that it was about time we had someone in charge who had actually won something; actually achieved something.

"To be fair, from what I can gather, Leeds did try and get Kendall but he turned them down . . . I can't say I blame him for that. I was a little surprised, and a little worried, when the news came through of Howard Wilkinson's appointment. Although he was doing well at Sheffield Wednesday at the time, he did have a reputation for using the route-one system. All I kept thinking was that he was going to transform Leeds into a sort of northern Wimbledon.

"I don't think the Leeds public would have taken to the long-ball game but I suppose they would have swallowed any resentment had it proved to be successful. Anyway, as it turned out, we didn't really have to worry because Wilkinson decided to join together the orthodox and the unorthodox. Sometimes we played the long ball, sometimes we didn't. It was a good system but, more importantly, it worked.

"The day we finally managed to escape from Division Two was wonderful. I couldn't get a ticket for the last fixture of the season at Bournemouth but it didn't really matter. You don't actually have to be present at an event to join in the celebrations, do you?

"Although I hoped that we would make an impression in the First Division, I didn't really expect too much because our side was inexperienced and certainly nowhere near as good as the likes of Liverpool and Arsenal. I would have settled for survival during that first season but, to my amazement, we did really, really well. Finishing in fourth place was a great achievement.

"Even though we had re-established ourselves as a leading club, I didn't think we had much chance of winning the title. If I am honest, I have to say that I still didn't think we had much chance of winning the title with three weeks of the season left. Manchester United should have won it. I don't think they are a better footballing side than Leeds but their squad was so much bigger and so much stronger than ours. I was totally amazed when they lost those games against Nottingham Forest and West Ham United; I really couldn't believe it.

"Once we had got our noses back in front I thought we'd do it. I thought we would settle for a draw against Sheffield United at Bramall Lane but I *knew* Manchester United would lose to Liverpool at Anfield. It had to be.

"It is still a little difficult to really believe that Leeds United are Football League Champions once again. We owe Howard Wilkinson so very much. The only problem now is staying at the top. We do need new players. I would like to see a really top-class striker brought to Elland Road – someone like Alan Shearer or even Dean Saunders.

"The important thing is not to let the momentum slip. We are back at the top of the pile and we want to stay there. Liverpool have proved that it can be done. Next season? I would settle for the League again plus one of the major cups, preferably the European Cup. I think we are all starting to believe that anything is possible once again.

RAY FELL (Chairman of the Leeds United Supporters Club):
"I have been the chairman of the supporters club for four years now which, I suppose, is the logical culmination of more than 40 years following the club through the good times and through the not so good times.

"I first watched Leeds United just after the Second World War. It was only the odd game, here and there, in the beginning but I quickly found myself becoming firmly attached to the club. It quickly became my main hobby. Those younger supporters who for so long bemoaned the club's lack of success after we had dropped down into the

Second Division in 1982 should have been around in those very early days. There wasn't a great deal to get excited about, believe me.

"I was one of those people who started life standing on the Kop; one of those who used to look across at those supporters in the seats and shake my head in disbelief. I couldn't see how they could possibly enjoy watching football whilst sitting down. Needless to say, my attitude towards the creature comforts began to change as I got older and now I have a place in the stand.

"It is not only difficult to believe what has happened to Leeds United Football Club over the past three seasons, it is also very difficult for someone like me to put it into words. When Liverpool's Mark Walters scored that second goal at Anfield to confirm Manchester United's defeat, I just couldn't believe it. I was in a daze, and even a week later I was still walking on clouds.

"Since the League Championship was clinched many, many people have asked me if I ever thought I would see this day again. That is another very tricky question because if I was to say 'no' it would sound like an admission of defeat; it would sound as though I had lost my faith. Let's put it this way, I always hoped that, one day, we would find ourselves back at the very top but during the problem days of the Eighties, I suppose that is all it was, hope.

"Football is a game of swings and roundabouts. If you want success you must be patient. Everything in life moves around in circles, even sport. Even when things were at their very bleakest back in 1988 when we were struggling near the foot of the Second Division table, I never surrendered my hope. I just thought that we needed a lucky break, something to spark us off.

"It would be very easy for me to sit here in the warm after-glow of a marvellous success and point an accusing finger at those men who tried, but failed, to put this great club back on the road to recovery and success. The important thing to remember is that managers like Allan Clarke, Eddie Gray and Billy Bremner gave everything they had. They had played for Leeds United, indeed all three were great servants. This club was very much a part of their life and I know, all too well, just how desperate they were to turn things around. They craved success just like we did.

"In many ways it was very sad that it did not work out for any of them because the Leeds public so wanted one of them to pull it off. I think Jack Charlton actually hit the nail on the head when he said that the problem was that managers were coming in and attempting to play attractive football from the word go – possibly in the Revie style which they knew and which they understood. The problem was that before you can turn on the style you have to have a set of talented and experienced footballers. Sadly, Clarke, Gray and Bremner did not have such a squad at their disposal.

"I particularly enjoyed watching Gray's team because while they were young they played some lovely football. I had great hopes for Bremner and, to be fair to him, he very nearly won promotion for us. Strange as it may seem, I think it is a good job we did not return to Division One under him. His team wasn't particularly strong and I doubt that we would have survived amongst the élite.

"I welcomed the appointment of Howard Wilkinson because I saw him as a more than useful manager with a very single-minded approach to football. After he had taken Leeds to the Second Division Championship, I really thought he could do something for us but even I am surprised at the speed of all this. To think that just three and a half years ago we were languishing near the bottom of Division Two. You have to pinch yourself, don't you!

"The biggest compliment which I can pay Mr Wilkinson is to say that he arrived here and did exactly what all the supporters wanted him to do – he took Leeds United by the scruff of the neck. I think he realised that you stand little or no chance of getting out of the Second Division by playing neat and pretty football. Naturally, all supporters want to see that from their team but you have to be realistic in this game and, if nothing else, Howard Wilkinson is very much a realist.

"He had a job to do and he set about doing that job in the best possible way. He added steel to the first-team squad and got the side playing in a way which was very difficult to combat. He made the players of Leeds United winners again. He also proved himself to be a very, very shrewd operator within the transfer market.

"Our big problem now is staying at the top. Even so, that is a very nice problem to have. Better that than having the problem of either getting out of the Second Division or fighting to avoid the drop from the First. I am very confident that if Howard is given the financial resources which all leading managers require, we will go from strength to strength. Hopefully, this will only be the beginning for us.

"It is funny, you know, I do actually feel a measure of sympathy for the supporters of Manchester United at this point. They had been the clear favourites all season and I know just how much they wanted that title. I actually thought they were going to get it after we were beaten 4–0 by Manchester City at Maine Road. I thought that was the turning point; I thought our chance had finally gone. I suspect that many of the Leeds players also thought that it had slipped away. Thinking about it now, that defeat may have helped us because I am sure that the players were a great deal more relaxed in the games which followed.

"I thought the title was definitely on its way to Old Trafford. I couldn't believe it when they lost those crucial games against Nottingham Forest and West Ham United; I really couldn't. Some people have been suggesting that Leeds United won the Championship by default. That simply isn't true. It is also very unfair. As far as I am concerned, the best team *always* wins the First Division title.

"I am so pleased for the club's supporters. They have displayed great loyalty and astonishing patience over the past few years and they really do deserve this moment of triumph.

"Personally, I can see no point at all in attempting to draw comparisons between the current Leeds team and the more famous team of 1974. Where does it get you? I suppose it was inevitable that people should start to liken Wilkinson to Revie but, while there are similarities, they are different in many ways. Both the 1974 side and this side are very, very good. The main difference is that the Seventies side was crammed full of international players. At the moment, that is not the case with Wilkinson's side but it could well happen in the next two or three years.

"Although Leeds United was an unfashionable club for so long, I do believe that very many people in this country are genuinely pleased at this success. Shortly after we had been confirmed as League Champions, I was sitting in the supporters' club when the telephone started ringing. Those calling with their congratulations were not exiled Leeds United fans but supporters of Liverpool. They were literally queuing up to say well done.

"Now, I know that they were delighted their old rivals, Manchester United, had failed to lift the title but I got the distinct feeling that they were pleased for us also. It was a touching and warming moment for me: something I shall not forget in a hurry."

ERIC ROSS (aged 35, accounts recovery supervisor, British Gas):
"Although my life-long allegiance to Leeds United has not wavered once over the past 25 years or so, I had begun to accept second-best as a way of life.

"Football supporters are often criticised for their apparent lack of patience yet all they ever ask is that their team run out on a Saturday afternoon, or a Wednesday night, and give everything they have for the club which pays their wages. It would be totally wrong of me to suggest that this has not always been the case at Leeds United over the past few years yet sometimes, I must confess, I began to wonder why I bothered driving all over the country to watch a team which so often seemed to be lacking in any discernible passion.

"Several times I returned home from matches so angry at what I had seen that I uttered the immortal phrase, 'Never again'. Inevitably, the following weekend I was back on the terraces screaming encouragement at those very players who had so annoyed me in the previous fixture.

"Until now, I have never believed in the old saying which suggests that every dog has its day. I thought we'd forever been confined to football's basement and that success would constitute the occasional good run in either the FA Cup or the League Cup.

"Before the arrival of Howard Wilkinson, things were getting so bad that I had started to set my sights, not on promotion back to the First Division, but on staving off the threat of relegation to the Third Division. We were constantly being told that the only way was up and that a brighter future was just around the next corner, yet I couldn't see any signs of this at all. Even if we had improved by 100 per cent during the period between 1986 and 1988, the very best we could have hoped for was promotion followed immediately by relegation. It just wasn't any fun following Leeds any more.

"Of course, I thought about packing it in but, then again, who didn't? Watching football in this day and age is a very expensive pastime, especially when you like to attend away games. A trip to, say, London or the south coast would cost at least £40 and I began to wonder if it was all worth it.

"While I have nothing but praise for the manner in which the club's directors have handled matters over the past three and a half years, I must question the wisdom of so many of their decisions stretching right back to 1974 when the late Don Revie severed his ties with Elland Road. I have the utmost respect for Brian Clough; he has proved himself to be one of the all-time greats of English football, yet I have to ask why he was placed in charge of a team which he had openly criticised right up to the very second he was appointed?

"I got the distinct impression that Clough was jealous of what Leeds had achieved under Revie and was deter-mined to dismantle his predecessor's squad as quickly as was possible. It may be true that the great Leeds team of that era was nearing the end of the line and that significant changes were called for but for a man to walk in and start stripping it bare on his first day was ridiculous and outrageous.

"It was obvious to everybody who cared for the club that the players would revolt and after what – 44 days was it? – Clough was sacked. Under the circumstances his successor, Jimmy Armfield, did a pretty good job. The lowest we finished during his four years in charge was tenth in Division One, which, while hardly spectacular, wasn't too bad. Once Armfield went we found ourselves saddled with two men of quite contrasting outlooks. Jock Stein didn't really seem too interested in the fortunes of Leeds United and left before most people realised he had arrived and Jimmy Adamson proved to be workmanlike but lacking in any real vision.

"I didn't actually believe that things could get much worse – but they did. In an attempt to placate a support which was draining away and becoming increasingly bitter and frustrated, the board threw itself into a sort of back-to-the-future policy. The idea seemed to be to give any former player a shot at managing the club. I wish someone had told the people who were in charge of Leeds United that good players do not always make good managers.

"Allan Clarke was full of totally silly boasts. 'We will win the European Cup within four years,' he declared. We were, in fact, relegated.

"Eddie Gray, one of the greatest players of his generation, was equally enthusiastic about the future of the club yet the best he achieved was a mid-table place in Division Two. Then it was goodbye Eddie, hello Billy.

"In my opinion, Billy Bremner has a great deal to answer for. Not only did he fail to arrest the slump in fortune but, more importantly, he sold some of the most promising players we had.

"While I do appreciate that hindsight is the most precise of sciences, it would be interesting to know why he sold the players he did. Andy Linighan was transferred to Oldham Athletic for £65,000. In 1990 he joined Arsenal from Norwich City for £1.25 million! Two other players who have proved themselves to be rather useful of late also went to Oldham – Andy Ritchie and Denis Irwin. At one stage I was tempted to buy a season ticket at Boundary Park!

"Any more? Sadly, yes. Terry Phelan, now valued at in excess of £1 million by Wimbledon, joined Swansea City on a free transfer, and Scott Sellars was 'stolen' by Blackburn Rovers for £20,000. At least Dick Turpin had the good grace to wear a mask when committing daylight robbery!

"Anyway, what is done is done. I know that Billy tried his best and with a little more good fortune could have taken us to promotion and to the FA Cup final in 1987. I know that he still attends games at Elland Road and despite my reservations about his managerial abilities, he will always be welcome, such was his contribution to our club's glorious past. Like most of my friends, I wasn't particularly overjoyed when it was announced that Howard Wilkinson had been appointed as manager. I suppose that was because we didn't really know a great deal about him. Deep down we all wanted a big name, someone who had won trophies.

"We do have some very talented players at Elland Road these days but the big difference is that we now have a manager who knows what he is doing. Wilkinson knew exactly what it was he wanted and he has achieved it. I didn't think it would be possible in such a short space of time but the man has proved me wrong – he's done it.

"The Sunday when we defeated Sheffield United and Liverpool hammered the final nail in Manchester United's title coffin will live with me forever. I was stunned when the whistle sounded at Anfield. I just stood there saying, 'We've done it'. Do I feel any sympathy for Manchester United? No, not really, although I must admit I did feel for their supporters when Ian Rush scored Liverpool's opening goal. As the television cameras focused in on Rush you could see the pain written across the faces of the United fans behind Schmeichel's goal. They knew that the Championship had gone; they knew their team had carelessly tossed away a golden opportunity which may not come again for several years.

"I didn't feel sorry for them for too long, though, and I never once felt sorry for the players at Old Trafford. When you get right down to it, football is a game which is all about supporters. They are the ones who suffer the biggest disappointments – not the players.

"For the first time since our team included the likes of Giles, Hunter, Charlton and Bremner, I can look to the future with optimism. Even if we were to finish next season empty-handed, I will at least know that my club is finally in very safe hands."

JOHN GOODYEAR (aged 33, catering salesman):
"In so many ways this is all very confusing because for years and years I have been turning up at Elland Road more in hope than expectation. Now, because we are League Champions, I shall arrive at the ground *expecting* a Leeds United victory and that can be a very dangerous thing to do.

"It is difficult to know where to begin. I suspect that if you had asked, four or five years ago, 1,000 of the club's supporters whether they thought something like this was possible, 999 of them would have said no chance. The one who said that, yes, he could foresee Leeds winning the Championship in 1992 would probably have been committed to a local hospital where the knives and forks were plastic.

"It is nice to be able to sit down and talk about the 'dark days' as though they were 10 or 15 years ago. Perhaps it is important that we do not lose sight of the fact that we were in dire trouble in the wrong half of the Second Division just three and a bit years ago. It hasn't taken very long for near-disaster to be turned into success but, I suppose, that sort of thing can work both ways. Who knows, in 1996 we might be back where we started?

"I would say that I reached my lowest ebb in the months before Howard Wilkinson took over. I was going to say that under Billy Bremner we were going nowhere but that's not true because we may well have ended up in the Third Division. Had that happened, I really don't know if I could have carried on supporting the club; you can only stretch loyalty so far and the thought of paying hard-earned cash to watch the likes of Chester City and Preston North End really did turn my stomach.

"Although I don't think Bremner was the right man for the job, it was always difficult to criticise him too much because we all knew he was trying his best to turn the club around. The same could be said of Allan Clarke and Eddie Gray. The problem was that no one at the club – in the board-room, I mean – seemed to appreciate that great players don't always make great managers. The supporters on the terrace seemed to come to grips with this fact a lot quicker than did our directors.

"I don't think anybody was particularly impressed with the news that Howard Wilkinson was to be the new manager. He hadn't really done much, had he? I think we were all looking for a Howard Kendall or even a Kenny Dalglish – someone who had achieved something, a big name to help lift the gloom.

"Anyway, to be fair to Howard – or the Messiah as we now like to refer to him – he has done a simply wonderful job and I think every supporter of Leeds United should get down on their knees to thank him, either that or we should all send him a five pound note.

"Howard just seemed to be able to do what the three . . . or four . . . or five . . . previous managers hadn't been able to do – he brought in the right sort of players and got them playing as a real team. There were a few eyebrows raised when he bought Vinnie Jones but even he was fun to have around for a while. I was even surprised that he bought Gordon Strachan because I thought he was finished. I'm now glad that Alex Ferguson thought the same thing. Silly, silly man!

"Even after we had won the Second Division Championship, I didn't really think we would make much of an impression in the top flight. I looked at the fixture list that first season back and thought, 'Oh my God . . . Liverpool, Arsenal, Manchester United, Spurs, Everton . . .' I just couldn't see us beating teams like that.

"After we had finished fourth I thought we'd do well to repeat that second time around. I never gave much thought to us actually winning the title. Why should I? Even after we had started the season so well, I still didn't think we were going to win it. I thought Manchester United were finally going to do it, something which made me feel quite ill. After we had been beaten by Manchester City, I was utterly convinced that it was all over. It had been fun, but it was definitely over. How wrong can you be?

"I am sure that result actually helped us because in the games which came immediately after that battering, the team played really well. On top of that we had Eric Cantona spinning his magic. My lasting memory of a great season is his goal against Chelsea at Elland Road. If that had been Mark Hughes or Ryan Giggs, it would probably have been acclaimed as the greatest individual goal of all time.

"The best thing about this whole thing is that it is now actually fun to go along to games. I used to turn up expecting little or nothing; now I turn up expecting great football, great goals and great results. It is still too expensive but at least I don't always feel that I have wasted my money. That is the way it used to be . . . five or six quid straight down the drain. Even when we lose I have the satisfaction of knowing that I have at least watched a Leeds team which *wants* to win and which *wants* to entertain.

"I think we've got some great players now, John Lukic should have been an England regular by now, David Batty and Gary McAllister are sheer quality and Lee Chapman and Rod Wallace always look like scoring. It is rather difficult not to get excited. I know that building up your hopes too much is a foolish thing to do but I just can't help it. I won't actually believe that we are the Champions of England until I see one of the top Continental sides appearing at Elland Road in the European Cup. That will really bring it all home to me.

"The only fear I have is that Howard Wilkinson will one day be tempted to leave and manage England. If Graham Taylor makes a mess of things – and there seems to be every indication he will – Howard is the obvious choice as his successor.

"Wouldn't that be just typical of our luck? We finally find a man who knows what he is doing and he is lured away by England. I can see that happening.

"Hopefully, our board will give Gordon Strachan a job on the coaching staff and then, if need be, he can follow in Howard's footsteps. If we try to do things as Liverpool have – promote from within – I think our future looks sound."

Chapter Eleven

THEY ALL HATE LEEDS – OR DO THEY?

Contrary to popular belief, watching professional football for a living hardly constitutes the "soft option" which many supporters – and wives and girlfriends – would believe.

Whenever a supporter manages to pierce the veil of secrecy which many sports journalists choose to hide behind, the inevitable first question asked is a simple one: "Do you get into matches for nothing?" The follow-up question depends on which part of the country you happen to reside in. If it is West Yorkshire you are asked: "Do you know Gordon Strachan and Eric Cantona?" If it is Merseyside it is: "Do you know Ian Rush and Neville Southall?" If you reply in the affirmative to both questions then you have either "got it made" or you have a "dream job the like of which I would give my right arm to do".

True, covering football at the highest level can be fun but every silver lining has a dark, foreboding cloud. During the course of an average season, a national sports writer can expect to cover anything between 80 and 110 matches. He, or she, will travel in excess of 25,000 miles and will be sustained by an endless diet of half-baked pies of no great quality and lukewarm tea.

Last season, for example, Oldham Athletic, a club noted for its hospitality, offered the assembled "hack pack" a half-time snack consisting of buns and carrot and orange soup during the game against Leeds United at Boundary Park.

Sometimes it would seem that no one likes the media. If a club is having a bad time, it is our fault. If a player is having a bad time, it is our fault. If a manager is having a bad time, it is our fault. The power of the pen is mightier than that of the boot etc . . .

The question is, do the media like Leeds United, the newly crowned champions of English football? Read on.

RICHARD BOTT (*Sunday Express*): "Leeds impressed me a great deal but I have to be honest and admit that I really didn't think they were going to win the Championship. When the season started, I would have listed them as, perhaps, third or fourth favourites behind the likes of Arsenal, Manchester United and, of course, Liverpool.

"They played some tremendous football, particularly in the weeks leading up to Christmas. Although they managed to keep themselves in contention I was absolutely convinced that their chance had gone in early April when they lost 4–0 against Manchester City at Maine Road.

"I was at that game and the looks on the faces of the Leeds players afterwards appeared to tell their own story. I think even they thought it had finally slipped away. I remember Gordon Strachan was asked if his team could still go on to take the title and he simply said: 'Well, I wouldn't put my mortgage on it.' I think that just about summed up the feeling in the Leeds dressing-room.

"Even Howard Wilkinson, who had remained optimistic throughout the entire campaign, had lost his usual sparkle. He said that his team would have to win most, if not all, of their remaining games if they were to stand a real chance. Had Manchester United not blown up in such spectacular fashion, I think he would have been proved correct.

"Let's face it – Manchester United laid down and died when it mattered the most. If they hadn't fallen to pieces in the final couple of weeks they would have won it. To be honest, I do believe that Manchester United, player for player, were a better team than Leeds. The one thing which Alex Ferguson's side could not match was Leeds' tremendous sense of spirit. They proved themselves to be a team in the truest form of the word.

"Bearing in mind that the Leeds squad was nothing like as strong as was the squad over at Old Trafford, I think they have done a marvellous job. Full credit must go to Howard Wilkinson for what is a great achievement. If you had said to me four years ago that Leeds United would be the 1991-1992 Football League Champions, I would probably have laughed long and loud.

"The thing which probably helped sustain Leeds was the absence of any real pressure. They weren't expected to win the title this season; I don't even think the players themselves were expecting to win it. I am certain that they had set their sights on claiming a place in the UEFA Cup – anything else was going to be a bonus.

"Of course, the reverse was true at Manchester United. They had been told by everybody that this was definitely going to be their season. Having to live up to expectations like that is exceedingly difficult. Leeds will find themselves faced by a similar level of expectancy next season and it will be interesting to see how they cope."

Most influential player? "**David Batty.** He really impressed me during the last few weeks of the season because he seemed to be getting stronger and more composed with every game. He produced four or five truly memorable displays towards the end which were vitally important because some of those around him had clearly begun to show signs of battle-fatigue.

"Batty is a good, solid player who can win the ball and then distribute it. One of his greatest attributes is his temperament, not so much in terms of discipline, more in terms of his mental approach to the game. At a time when the pressure was building up, he just got on with his job the best he could. I am sure that he will have a bright future at international level because, as he is getting older, he is getting better.

"Batty narrowly edged out John Lukic who had a tremendous season. If a side does not have a goalkeeper of proven ability and experience its chances of winning a major prize are greatly reduced."

PAUL HETHERINGTON (*News of the World*): "I believe that a great deal of the credit – quite possibly most of the credit – must go to Howard Wilkinson for totally transforming the fortunes of a club which, for so long, appeared to be going nowhere at all. Howard has done a fantastic job at Elland Road but, more importantly, he has done it very, very quickly. I don't think anyone ever had too many doubts about his managerial abilities but I think the speed with which he has turned around the fortunes of Leeds United has surprised a lot of people, both inside and outside of the game.

"At the end of every season, when the Manager of the Year is named, it is always awarded to the man who has led his club to the First Division title. Sometimes I think there are more deserving cases but on this occasion the award has definitely gone to the right man – Wilkinson is the manager of the year without a doubt.

"Like Arsenal and Liverpool before them, Leeds have won the title by playing attractive football. They entertained wherever they went and I don't think there will be too many people who would disagree with the notion that they are, indeed, worthy Champions.

"I was particularly impressed by them during the last two or three weeks of the season when the pressure was really on. After they had been heavily defeated by Queen's Park Rangers at Loftus Road and by Manchester City at Maine Road, it would have been easy for them to fold but they didn't. They kept plugging away, believing all the while that they still had a chance. Even when they were written off by the nation's bookmakers, they kept their cool and their patience.

"I thought their chance had gone several times. When they dropped valuable home points against Aston Villa and West Ham United, I just couldn't see them staying in touch with Manchester United at the top. They proved me wrong, though.

"Howard Wilkinson deserves great praise for the way in which he kept his players out of the limelight. He successfully shielded them from the pressure at the crucial times. There was never any boasting at Elland Road; they simply applied themselves to the tasks demanded by their manager.

"I think that even the most dedicated and loyal Leeds United fan would agree that Manchester United had the bigger – and better – first-team squad. Leeds thoroughly deserve to be League Champions.

"I always fancied Arsenal to retain their title. I waited patiently for them to launch a sustained bid but when it finally materialised it was just too late."

Most influential player? "**Gary Speed.** It was a very, very difficult choice because so many of the Leeds players have impressed me this season. Gordon Strachan, despite his injury problems, had another tremendous season in midfield where he is still such an influential player. John Lukic was a model of consistency and Tony Dorigo really enhanced his claims for a regular place in the England international team.

"In the end, I had to go for Speed because he is so good to watch. He has pace, great heading ability and he can beat defenders. On top of all that he is so versatile, as he proved towards the end of the campaign when he filled in at full-back. He could well turn out to be a modern-day Paul Madeley. I can pay him no higher compliment."

STEVE BIERLEY (*The Guardian*): "Let's face it, until Howard Wilkinson was appointed in 1988 after the dismissal of Billy Bremner, Leeds United was a club which was going nowhere fast.

"I have to be perfectly honest and admit that I did not think he was the right choice at all. I had never liked Sheffield Wednesday's style of play – it was far too direct for me; so predictable and tedious. During Leeds' Second Division Championship-winning season, I thought it was a case of Wednesday revisited. I wasn't impressed at all, although it is fair to say that few teams have ever managed to win promotion to the First Division by playing pretty football.

"However, once Leeds had arrived back in the big time they modified their previously unrefined style to stunning effect. I was genuinely surprised by the manner in which they approached their first season back in Division One. Most teams who had been languishing in the Second Division for many years would have been perfectly happy to consolidate their newly acquired position but Leeds wanted far more than that.

"Finishing fourth at the end of that season was a major achievement. Winning the League Championship after just two seasons is a remarkable achievement. Wilkinson, to his credit, has successfully blended together two quite differing styles and footballing ideologies. Leeds can now play cultured football and they can play direct football.

"The route-one style does have its advantages but only if it is allied to some basic, more orthodox, technique will it produce consistent results. In many ways, Leeds' football has been a revelation; one of the few bright spots in what was an otherwise largely undistinguished season.

"When Leeds won promotion I thought they might struggle. I couldn't see them being relegated but, there again, I couldn't see them winning trophies. I had so many reservations about Wilkinson's squad. I couldn't see Lee Chapman scoring many goals in the First Division. He has. I could see Mel Sterland struggling. He hasn't.

"It was during the FA Cup saga against Arsenal last season that I began to realise that Leeds were not too far off being a really useful side. Arsenal were formidable opponents but during the course of the four matches, Leeds matched them all the way.

"The key to this success undoubtedly has its roots in Wilkinson's signings during last summer. The arrival of players like Tony Dorigo, Steve Hodge and Rod Wallace added a touch of real quality to a senior squad which could already claim to be one of the strongest in the Football League. He bought very well did Mr Wilkinson.

"I still didn't think they would win the title, though. I thought that the serious injuries sustained by the likes of Chris Fairclough, Lee Chapman and Mel Sterland would result in their commendable challenge faltering. Again, I was to be proved wrong. Wilkinson simply stuck by the players he had, didn't rush out to try and find replacements and, significantly, didn't panic. I would have to agree with those people who say that Manchester United threw away the title because they really should have won it. But, Leeds kept going and they are worthy Champions.

"Interestingly, shortly after the season had finished I received a letter from someone living in Bradford who attended a sportsman's dinner in Huddersfield last winter. The guest speaker was Howard Wilkinson and when asked what it takes to win the League title, he replied: 'A minimum of 17 to 18 top-class players, each capable of dove-tailing into a certain formation when called upon to do so.' When asked how far he was from achieving this goal at Leeds United, he replied: 'A million light years.' He was wrong and I bet he is delighted."

Most influential player? "**Tony Dorigo.** He has made a great deal of difference to the balance of the side. He has taken so much pressure off Mel Sterland because Leeds now have two full-backs who are capable of coming forward to deliver crosses of great power and accuracy."

MARTIN LEACH (*News of the World*): "I think Howard Wilkinson is one of the few managers who has actually deserved to be named as the Manager of the Year. Personally, I feel it is diabolical that this prestigious award *always* goes to the manager of the League Champions but this time there can be no complaints; there can be no arguments.

"I actually find it rather difficult to praise Leeds United without, in a funny sort of way, sounding a little disrespectful. The plain truth of the matter is that they had less resources than Manchester United, less potential and an inferior squad. Having said that, they won it and they deserved to win it in the end.

"Amid all the jubilation which descended on Elland Road ater that enthralling Sunday when they beat Sheffield United and their biggest rivals lost to Liverpool at Anfield, I suspect there were people at the club walking around pinching themselves. I don't think there is any doubt that this success has come at least two years ahead of schedule. I don't think anybody at Leeds United – not Howard Wilkinson, not Leslie Silver – honestly thought that they would win the League Championship in only their second season back in the First Division. That sort of thing just isn't supposed to happen in English football any more.

"Leeds' biggest asset is their team spirit. They work together and they work for each other. Even when things looked decidedly bleak for them they never gave up; they simply rolled up their sleeves and dug in. I don't know whether they were really expecting Manchester United to slip up in such an alarming fashion but they gave the impression that they were.

"I can't really praise Howard Wilkinson enough. He never once let the obvious pressure seep through to his playing staff and he refused to tinker with his first team after it had proved its worth. That is something which cannot be said of every manager in the First Division because several seemed to derive great pleasure from disrupting a winning line-up.

"I actually think that John Giles hit the nail firmly on the head when he said that he regarded the current Leeds United side as 'highly motivated scramblers'. He didn't mean that in a derogatory sense at all but I know what he was getting at. They are, of course, much more than that because they have several players of the very highest quality in their side, people like David Batty, Gary McAllister, Gordon Strachan and Tony Dorigo.

"It takes far more than mere skill to win the biggest prize in English football and Leeds have far more than skill. I think Don Revie would have been very proud of them."

Most influential player? "**David Batty.** I was never a great fan of his before this season but he has really won me over. Although his contribution was sound all season long I shall never forget his performance during the 4–0 defeat by Manchester City at Maine Road in early April. It is sometimes the case that you learn far more about a player when things are going badly than you do when things are going according to plan. That was just such an occasion.

"I couldn't believe how well he played on that afternoon. He ran around like a man possessed, tackling, passing, shooting – it was incredible. Even when his team had fallen three goals behind, he didn't give up. He chased lost causes all afternoon. It was a phenomenal display of guts and character.

"I wouldn't say that he is the most creative player ever to feature in the midfield section for Leeds United but his capacity for sheer hard work is second to none. The biggest compliment which I can pay him is to say that I think he has got a better 'engine' than Bryan Robson, a man who for many years has been universally acclaimed as the modern game's ultimate competitor.

"He reminds me a great deal of Nobby Stiles in so much as he runs things in the middle of the park despite the fact that he is surrounded by players of superior technique. If he is used in the right way and within the right team framework, he is a brilliant player."

MICHAEL MORGAN (*The Sun*): "Despite what so many people have said over the past few weeks there is no doubt in my mind that Leeds United thoroughly deserve to be the League Champions – no doubt at all. I don't quite understand why it is that certain individuals, both inside and outside the game, have been attempting to lessen their achievement. How on earth you can successfully devalue something like this is beyond me. As Howard Wilkinson said many times after his team had been confirmed as Champions, all his players could do was go out, do their very best and win the thing. They did that and yet still people insist on hinting that they are in some way second-class winners.

"To lift the Championship you still have to play 42 very tough games and you still have to prove yourself to be the very best. There are no easy routes to success in English football. True, people can say that the First Division isn't at its strongest, that certain teams were unlucky, that other teams suffered from bad injury problems – they can say all that but it still should not be allowed to detract from what is a wonderful, and quite remarkable, achievement.

"The other theory which has abounded since Liverpool finally killed off the challenge of Manchester United at Anfield is that Leeds won it by default rather than on merit. Again, that is groundless rubbish. The best team will *always* win the title. Those who say that Alex Ferguson's team handed the title to Leeds United on a plate should take a good look at the final First Division table. The proof is there, for all to see, in black and white.

"Leeds won more games than any other side, lost fewer games than any other side and won it by four clear points – not on goal difference or by virtue of having scored more times – by four clear points. Now, in my book, that is an emphatic victory.

"People can say that Manchester United threw away silly points but you can quite easily say the same of Leeds. Just look at the home games against Aston Villa, Southampton and West Ham United for example.

"One of the main reasons why Leeds once again find themselves at the very top of English football is their manager, because Howard Wilkinson is one of the shrewdest operators in the Football League. When he left Sheffield Wednesday for Elland Road back in 1988 most people acknowledged that he was a more than capable manager but there did seem to be a rather large question mark over his ability to select the right players when dealing within the transfer market. I think he has proved his worth over the past three and a half years by buying quality footballers like John Lukic, Tony Dorigo, Gordon Strachan – the list is endless if you think about it. In fact, I think it is safe to say that not one of those players he has brought in has flopped or let anyone down. That, in itself, is quite a remarkable achievement.

"If everything goes according to plan, Leeds should now be in a position to build upon this success and move forward with great confidence. Wilkinson now knows exactly what it takes to win the game's biggest prizes and, I am sure, he will have learned a great deal over the past 12 months or so. He will know what he needs, in the shape of new talent, to keep his club at the very top of English football and he will know which departments he will be required to strengthen if his side is to make an impact in the European Cup next term.

"During the course of a long and arduous season there are bound to be several moments which can later be isolated as significant but I believe that the outcome of the trilogy of games against Manchester United over the Christmas and New Year period was the real turning point for both clubs. Although Manchester United must have been absolutely delighted with the way those three games went for them, it left them with so much to do. I suppose it is quite ironic, in a way, that Manchester United should ultimately become the victims of their own success because that had happened to Don Revie's Leeds team so many times during the late Sixties and early Seventies.

"Once it became clear that Ferguson's team would be faced by a back-log of fixtures in the final few weeks of the season, I really did begin to fancy Leeds' chances. It doesn't matter how good a side is, playing four important games in just six days is a very tall order.

"The other important factor was the way in which Wilkinson coped with the pressure as it began to build up after Christmas. He never once gave the impression that he was worried, nervous or apprehensive but inside he must have been shaking with the excitement of it all. By remaining outwardly calm, I am certain that he helped his players a great deal. That is management of the very highest order.

"There are so many factors which come into play here. Gordon Strachan must go down as one of the greatest signings of all time – not just where Leeds United are concerned, but generally. He might now start to diminish as a player because of his advancing years but his influence will be felt within the dressing-room for just so long as he is at Elland Road.

"While I wouldn't openly criticise the Leeds board for the appointments of former players like Allan Clarke, Eddie Gray and Billy Bremner – three men who were totally committed to the Leeds United cause – I do think they were right in trying to sever their links with the past – with the Don Revie era. It really did need an outsider to come in and sweep the club clean. There was a desperate need for a fresh beginning and Wilkinson was the right man for what was a difficult job.

"You just can't afford to live in the past if you are to prosper in this sport. While ever Leeds had a manager who was remembered as a great player, comparisons were inevitable. Teams like the one which Revie assembled come along once in a lifetime – if you are lucky.

"Things have changed so much over the past two decades. You can no longer whistle down the nearest mine-shaft and expect a team of proficient players to emerge. The days of teams being crammed full of home-town boys is most definitely over. Kids these days have other interests apart from football. If you want the best players, you have to go out and find them. You have to scour Europe and then back up your instincts with hard cash. That is what Howard Wilkinson has done and it has worked."

Most influential player? "**Gordon Strachan.** I could have picked any one of ten or eleven players, really. Leeds have the best English-born goalkeeper in John Lukic. They have several players right out of the top drawer in men like Tony Dorigo, Gary Speed, and Gary McAllister. They have unsung heroes in Chris Whyte and Chris Fairclough.

"In the end it has to be Strachan simply because of his massive influence, both on and off the field of play. He is a brilliant footballer, a model professional and a shining example to all youngsters."

JOHN EDWARDS (*Daily Mirror*): "I am really delighted for Leeds United and that is something coming from someone who spent his formative years standing on the Stretford End watching Manchester United!

"This was ultimately a triumph of one man's nerve, that man being Howard Wilkinson, of course. Yes, it is the players who win the games, who take the knocks and who receive the accolades but it is debatable whether the greatest set of footballers ever assembled would achieve very much unless they had a brilliant manager to guide them from the touchline.

"If the battle for the League Championship is looked at as a two-horse race – which it was until the last few weeks of the season – it is important that people analyse the contribution of the two managers, Wilkinson and his opposite number, Alex Ferguson.

"From a neutral standpoint, the two men are completely different both in terms of natural character and in terms of how they dealt with the obvious pressure of attempting to lead their clubs to the title. Ferguson, good manager that he obviously is, always seemed to be a bag of nerves; he seemed to be on edge all the time. On top of that he is one of the more volatile managers within the English game, something which can, occasionally, work to a team's advantage.

"Wilkinson, on the other hand, was so laid-back about everything. He just got on with his job of work very quietly and kept his cool. I'll never forget an incident before the FA Cup, third-round tie against Manchester United at Elland Road.

"On the morning of the match, my newspaper had printed a piece by the former Liverpool defender, Emlyn Hughes, in which he had been . . . how shall I put it . . . none too complimentary about Leeds United. Howard had obviously seen the piece and he was not amused in the slightest. As I made my way up the main staircase at Elland Road, he called me over and explained in great detail why he was disgusted by the tone of the article. Our conversation then drifted on to various other topics relating to tabloid journalism. I couldn't believe that a man who was less than 20 minutes away from one of the most important games of his season could so divorce himself from proceedings and enter into such a detailed discussion. It was like the two of us were chatting over a pint on a Sunday lunchtime.

"I think that possibly Manchester United were slightly the better of the two teams but that Leeds had more character and more nerve when it really mattered the most. It became clear around February that the fight for the title was going to go down to the wire. If that does happen, it is usually the team with the stronger will to win which carries the day. With two weeks of the season left to go, I was utterly convinced that the title was going to go to Old Trafford. Friends and relations kept asking me for my 'expert opinion' and I just had to say it was going to be Manchester United's Championship. So much happened in those final few days that it did take a while for it all to sink in. I am certain that thousands of Leeds United supporters were still checking the final

First Division table for days afterwards just to make sure that they hadn't been dreaming.

"I think the part which has been played by the key members of the Leeds board has been slightly over-looked in recent weeks. Chairmen are usually criticised and only rarely praised. On this occasion at least, Leslie Silver, the Leeds chairman, deserves applauding because but for his vision of a brighter, more successful future for his club, none of this would probably have happened.

"His decision to appoint Howard Wilkinson was a bold one. His decision to hand over a great deal of money to enable his manager to buy new players was even bolder. It was a gamble but one which has paid off handsomely. Sure, it was Wilkinson who went out and found the quality players who transformed Leeds United's fortunes but it was Leslie Silver, along with Bill Fotherby, who sanctioned the deals. They both deserve great credit for thinking big at a time when the club was in a bad shape."

Most influential player? "**Gary McAllister.** The balance in the Leeds midfield was absolutely crucial and the relationship between McAllister and David Batty was tremendous. They complemented each other's play so well; they just gelled together as though they had been playing alongside each other all their lives.

"McAllister is a class act and, bearing in mind he only cost £1 million, he was a bargain. He should, perhaps, score a few more goals but he is something of a rarity amongst cultured midfielders in that he really loves to get stuck in.

"I could have picked anyone, to be honest. John Lukic was brilliant, Tony Dorigo was excellent and Gordon Strachan was his usual efficient self. It is difficult to pick one player out because Leeds United are a team. That is their great strength and that is why it is they, and not Manchester United, who are Champions of England."

CHRIS WILSON (*Daily Star*): "In the end it all boils down to a personal triumph for Howard Wilkinson over his chief rival, Alex Ferguson. Perhaps that is an over-simplistic view but when everything is taken into account, I believe the deciding factor was quite probably the management of Wilkinson.

"There is no doubt that there was a prolonged psychological battle between the two men – especially in the last few weeks of the season – and there is no doubt that Wilkinson won that war hands down.

"After Leeds' final League game against Norwich City, he openly confessed that, back in August, before a ball had been kicked, he felt that he had the fourth-strongest squad in the First Division after Manchester United, Liverpool and Arsenal. I would have to agree totally with that assessment.

"So why did Leeds finish on top? That will be a question which Ferguson, Graeme Souness and George Graham will have asked themselves a thousand and one times over the past few months. If the League Championship was always won by the club which has the biggest, most experienced squad then the title would definitely have gone to Old Trafford this season. If you look at the Leeds squad and at the Manchester United squad there really is no comparison. Ferguson had so many top-class players at his disposal that he could have named two attractive-looking teams most Saturday mornings. Leeds, on the other hand, seemed to use the same 14 or 15 players for the entire season.

"Even when Wilkinson lost key players through injury – Chris Fairclough, Lee Chapman, Tony Dorigo etc – he refused to panic. He didn't rush out and waste his money on replacements of dubious ability. Even when the title seemed to be slipping away from him, Wilkinson didn't seek to change things. He kept faith with those players who had served him so well during the early part of the season.

"His attitude towards the end of the campaign was tremendous. He looked at what was happening at the top of the table, looked at what he had available to him and kept on naming the same team. This explains why a player of Eric Cantona's obvious ability could not lay claim to a regular first-team place as the season began to near its thrilling climax.

"The complete opposite seemed to be true over at Old Trafford. Alex Ferguson just didn't seem to know what his best team was. Players like Neil Webb, Mark Hughes, Lee Sharpe and Andrei Kanchelskis were dropped, recalled, dropped and recalled. There just didn't seem to be any real continuity which is something, I believe, you must have if you are to win the Championship. Constantly changing the make-up of a side is fine in cup football – horses for courses, you could say – but not in the League.

"In the final count, Wilkinson simply out-thought and out-manoeuvred his opposite number. It was all about nerve in those final few weeks and the players of Leeds United proved themselves to be both mentally and physically strong. It is often the case that managers are given far too much credit but that cannot be said on this particular occasion."

Most influential player? "**Gordon Strachan.** He was magnificent up until about January when the wear and tear of a long season started to take its toll. Even when he was out through injury, his influence could still be felt.

"His enthusiasm and speed of thought was absolutely essential and in those final few weeks he brought to bear his immense experience. At £300,000 he must go down as one of the biggest bargains in the history of British football."

RUSSELL THOMAS (*The Guardian*): "Ironically, the first time I saw Leeds was against Crystal Palace at Selhurst Park when they slipped to their first defeat of the season. The fact that they deserved at least a draw on that night is now something of an irrelevance but even at that early stage I felt that they would lose fewer games than their major rivals. It was nothing more than a gut feeling – a natural instinct – but they were so well organised that I suspected they would go on to enjoy a highly successful season.

"What particularly impressed me was the sense of balance in midfield. They passed the ball around with great economy of effort and their flexibility in the centre of the park presented them with so many different options.

"Every time I saw them – which was mostly away from Elland Road – they were very positive in their outlook.

Even on foreign soil they did not hesitate to attack the game.

"I do not believe that they have been given full credit for what they have achieved. To win the Second Division Championship and then the League Championship itself within the space of two years is quite remarkable.

"They have players of great quality in their side, players who will improve as they become more experienced. Tony Dorigo was a most inspired buy and in Gary McAllister they have arguably the best passer of a ball in the English game. Gary Speed is a wonderful talent. At present I believe him to be one of the best in the country but if he continues to make progress, I think he may well establish himself as a truly great footballer. He certainly has the all-round ability.

"Several of the Leeds players have been ridiculously underestimated by certain sections of the media. Lee Chapman's goals-per-game ratio is magnificent and apart from his largely unproductive spell at Arsenal, he has enjoyed a tremendous career. Mel Sterland is another unsung hero. His contribution throughout the season was crucially important.

"I think the most interesting thing is that Leeds have won the title with two footballing centre-backs which is certainly something of a rarity these days. I rate both Chris Whyte and Chris Fairclough very highly indeed. In fact, I would have no hesitation in placing Whyte in my list of top five players of the season.

"In a way, the fact that Howard Wilkinson had such a small squad at his disposal may well have worked in his favour because it meant that he always had a good idea what his best side was. Small can be beautiful, sometimes.

"In the days which followed Leeds' installation as the new Football League Champions several of this country's leading sports journalists attempted to draw comparisons between the club's current side and famous sides of the past and the not-too-distant past.

"It was suggested that only a handful of Wilkinson's players would have been able to force their way into the Arsenal side which won the title in 1990-91 or into Don

Revie's famous team of the Seventies. I disagreed with most of these comparisons. The current Leeds team is exceptionally strong and exceptionally talented. I enjoyed watching them a great deal and they deserve this success."

Most influential player? "**Chris Whyte.** He had a simply superb season even if his form did start to dip a little towards the end of the campaign. He is quick, good in the air and very comfortable on the ball. His partnership with Chris Fairclough was crucial to the development of Leeds as a footballing side."

DAVID WALKER (*Daily Mail*): "I do honestly believe that Leeds United's season would have been hailed as a success whether they had won the League Championship or not. It didn't really matter what the final outcome was because Howard Wilkinson had already achieved something far bigger – something of far greater significance – in that he finally succeeded in removing the stigma which had been attached to the club's name for the best part of 20 years.

"Since the days of the late Don Revie, Leeds had been regarded as dour, uncompromising and over-physical. It really didn't seem to matter that several of the club's teams between, say, 1976 and 1988 had played some very attractive football. It was still a case of 'dirty Leeds' or 'we all hate Leeds'. Nothing, it would seem, could alter people's perception of Leeds United.

"Even when Leeds played well, the appreciation of their efforts was grudging, forced and delivered with a degree of reluctance which many, many people found unacceptable.

"When Howard Wilkinson took over from Billy Bremner in 1988, the club's disciplinary record was very, very poor. In an attempt to force their way back into the First Division, Leeds had added far too much steel and aggression to their football. The result was a Football Association fine which was hanging over the club when the new manager took office. No one has mentioned that particular problem in the past three and a half years because it no longer exists – Leeds, under Wilkinson, have cleaned up their act to such an extent that they are now rightly regarded as one of the fairest sides in the Football League.

"More importantly, they are now regarded as one of the most attractive and entertaining sides in the Football League. The days when the name Leeds United was synonymous with dull, negative football spiced with rather unpleasant undertones have gone. Wherever Leeds have played over the past couple of seasons they have won rich applause not only for the commendable quality of their football but also for the spirit with which they perform. This is surely Howard Wilkinson's greatest achievement. Now, even the club's most vociferous critics can be found singing their praises. It is quite possible that the current side is actually receiving a far better press than did Don Revie's more famous – and more ruthless – side. The whole image of the club has been transformed and with the Leeds supporters also beginning to win a measure of respectability within football, the future does look unquestionably bright.

"Although many people believe that the turning point in Leeds' season came around Christmas after Manchester United had removed most of the obstacles in their path by eliminating them from both the FA Cup and the Rumbelows League Cup, I would beg to differ. The crucial moment, the massive psychological blow, came on Easter Monday shortly after they had defeated Coventry City at Elland Road.

"What I am talking about has nothing to do with that win returning Leeds to the top of the table following Manchester United's defeat, earlier in the day, by Nottingham Forest. That was obviously very important but the key incident came in the dressing-room afterwards.

"Having discussed this with several of the Leeds players, I now know that Wilkinson walked in, turned to his team, said, 'Well done', and then congratulated them all on their achievement. The achievement in question was not defeating Coventry City, nor was it climbing back above their closest rivals. The achievement was having definitely qualified for a place in the UEFA Cup the following season. That had been their manager's primary objective all along and it had been attained.

"He then said that anything else would be a real bonus for both him and his board of directors. I do honestly believe this was a master-stroke because the players must have felt any pressure simply drain away. Wilkinson is a demanding man but they had pleased him. What is more, they could now go out, free from worry, and try and give him the ultimate prize.

"Because even Wilkinson had never really thought in terms of Leeds becoming League Champions just two years after being in the Second Division, there was never any *real* pressure at Elland Road. Leeds were not expected to win the title so, if they did, it would be a bonus.

"That was most certainly not the case over at Old Trafford. After Manchester United had beaten Barcelona in Rotterdam to win the European Cup Winners Cup at the end of last season, Alex Ferguson immediately said that winning cup competitions was fine but that he wanted the League title. He said that the League would be the priority in the following season; that everything would be geared to returning the title to the club after an absence of 25 years.

"I believe that put his players under a great deal of pressure even before the season had started. I just wonder if everyone at Old Trafford became a little too single-minded about the whole thing. Winning the Championship had become an obsession and if you are obsessed with something it goes without saying that you are under pressure.

"I am delighted that Leeds have won the Championship because they fully deserved to. I am more delighted that people's opinion of the club itself has changed so dramatically for the better.

"I remember distinctly one occasion back in 1982 which placed neatly into perspective the ill-feeling which at one time threatened to totally envelop the club. I was sitting at a Football Writers Association dinner on the night Leeds were playing their final fixture of the 1981-82 season against West Bromwich Albion at The Hawthorns. Leeds' relegation from the First Division was confirmed by a 2–0 defeat and when that result was announced midway through the evening there was a roar of approval and a spontaneous round of applause from the so-called neutral guests.

"This year, after Howard Wilkinson had picked up the major award at the Barclay's Manager of the Year ceremony, reference was made to Leeds' recent revival. This time there was sustained and genuinely warm applause. That illustrates graphically exactly what Howard Wilkinson has achieved."

Most influential player? "**Chris Whyte** and **John Lukic**. I am sorry but I just can't separate the two. John has had a fantastic season, keeping 20 clean sheets throughout the League campaign. Whyte is one of the great unsung heroes."

BARRY FOSTER (*Yorkshire Post*): "I think that it is fair to say that I have been covering Leeds United for longer than any other sports writer, having started watching them on a regular basis when I joined the *Yorkshire Post* back in the 1967-68 season.

"Back in the Sixties, when the late Don Revie had fashioned the side which won promotion from the Second Division, I used to talk about fairy stories in terms of Leeds United coming from nowhere to contest the game's biggest prizes. Well, the fairy story has happened again – twice in one lifetime.

"When Revie's famous side came to the end of the line and Leeds sank out of the European scene, it was rather like someone throwing a glass of cold water in my face. Although Leeds did re-emerge as a force to be reckoned with towards the end of the Seventies, the last decade has been a fairly grey area with regard to covering football in Yorkshire.

"The great joy for me now is not only the transformation which has swept Leeds United back into a position of prominence but the re-awakening of the whole county. We have Leeds United as Football League Champions, Sheffield Wednesday finishing in third place and gaining entry to the UEFA Cup, Sheffield United in the top ten and last, but not least, Middlesbrough back in the First Division. From a position where Yorkshire football was seemingly going nowhere we have four clubs in Division One and real potential at places like Huddersfield Town and Rotherham United. It is like having all my birthdays at once.

"If you are looking to isolate the reasons behind the renaissance of Leeds United you need look no further than the manager, Howard Wilkinson, and the meticulous way he goes about his business. While I do not believe the present side to be anything like as good as Revie's famous team of the late Sixties and early Seventies, I think that many of the comparisons which have been made of late are very unfair. If people do have to make these comparisons then they should compare Wilkinson's side with the Leeds side which won promotion to the First Division in 1964. That is the only way you can do it.

"To be honest, I do believe that the current side is better than Revie's early team; it has more class about it. The important thing to remember is that the current side does have something which the team of '64 did not have – they have history upon which to build and prosper. Before Revie succeeded in making Leeds United a household name, there was no pedigree at the club; before Don Revie there was nothing.

"The one fair comparison which can be made is, perhaps, between the two managers. Revie was a careful thinker and a very good planner and so too is Wilkinson.

"Bearing in mind that Manchester United not only had more potential than did Leeds but also far greater resources, I think they should have won the Championship this year. Having said that, I always had a sneaking feeling that they would trip up in the final straight just as had Leeds United so many times in the past.

"With ten games to go, I volunteered to forecast the results for the leading seven clubs in the First Division with a view to predicting who would eventually come out on top. In general terms the idea paid off because I correctly placed six out of the seven – with Leeds United on top. I actually had them as Champions by virtue of goal difference so they ended the season in slightly better style than I had been anticipating.

157

"It really is wonderful to have them back in the mainstream of English football."

DON WARTERS (*Evening Post*, Leeds): Having spent the last 25 years covering the fortunes – and misfortunes – of Leeds United, I had begun to seriously question whether I would ever see this day again. Although I had begun to suspect that Howard Wilkinson was definitely on the verge of transforming the club, I have to admit that I am very surprised by the speed of change. It is remarkable to think that just over three years ago the club was struggling to hold its own in the Second Division. The prospect of winning the League Championship seemed a million miles away at the time.

"I was delighted when it was announced that Wilkinson was to succeed Billy Bremner back in 1988 because I did think he was the right man for what was a difficult task. Although he had never really proved himself at the top level, that could possibly be put down to the fact that he was working within a very restrictive financial framework at Sheffield Wednesday. What had impressed me was the progress he had made during his time at Notts County. He had done an exceptional job at a small and unfashionable club.

"I was told at the time that if Leeds were looking for someone to lead them out of the Second Division then Wilkinson was definitely the right man. Thankfully, the club's directors were obviously in full agreement with that particular line of thought.

"It was after he had taken Leeds back into the First Division that I began to feel he was on the right track; he seemed to be a manager who knew exactly what he was doing and exactly where it was he wanted his club to go.

"I didn't expect them to win the title this year. Even as the season began to near its climax, I still felt that Manchester United would triumph in the end. I was wrong and I couldn't be more pleased about it.

"If people are looking for turning points I think you would have to go back to the game against Liverpool at Anfield. At that point, Leeds were trailing Manchester United and their prospects did not look at all good. They managed to pick up a point from a goalless draw but, in truth, I wasn't too happy about that because I felt they should have gone hell for leather in search of victory. Howard was pleased, though, and said that it would prove to be a valuable result. He was right.

"The other key moment may have been the crushing defeat by Manchester City at Maine Road because Leeds played a great deal better afterwards. Perhaps they thought their chance had gone and they simply relaxed.

"Whilst the drawing of comparisons between the current Leeds team and Don Revie's famous side of the Seventies is inevitable, I wouldn't even bother attempting to compare them. It is unfair and pointless. Leeds' problem now – nice problem that it is – is staying at the top of English football. When they won promotion, Gordon Strachan said that the really hard work was still to come. Even now, after this tremendous success, I am certain that he would say the same thing. They are Champions but they must now prove themselves to be worthy Champions and that will not be easy at all.

"I do feel that this latest Championship success has created far more interest within the city than did the last one in 1974. The city was buzzing with excitement for weeks afterwards. On the Monday after the title had been clinched, newsagents sold out of the *Evening Post* within minutes of it being delivered. People were so anxious to get hold of a copy, presumably as a souvenir, that they began to queue outside shops in readiness for the arrival of our second edition. Believe me, that sort of thing doesn't happen very often."

Most influential player? "**David Batty.** He was a key figure within a very effective midfield section.

"If I had to select the man who has had the greatest effect over the past three years then it would be Gordon Strachan because his influence, both on and off the field of play, has been immense. As a club man no one compares to him.

"It is difficult to pick out one individual because the important thing is that Howard Wilkinson has built a team. They all play for each other and there is no real star."

WILLIAM JOHNSON (*Daily Telegraph*): "Like most people, I would assume that Howard Wilkinson's only thoughts upon being appointed Leeds manager back in 1988 were on assembling a team which was sufficiently competent to escape from the Second Division. Having done that in next to no time, I am reasonably sure that he will have been very surprised at the impact which the nucleus of that team was to make on the First Division.

"To finish in fourth place at the end of a season which, presumably, was all about simple consolidation was a tremendous achievement. Inevitably, Howard will have stretched the parameters of his ambition as he prepared for the following season and he will have been looking for a European place. Whether or not he actually believed (or dared believe) that his team was actually good enough to win the League Championship itself is another matter.

"To improve the chances of qualifying for the UEFA Cup he spent a considerable amount of money but the important thing is that he spent it very wisely indeed. He added quality to a squad which was already amongst the strongest in the English game.

"Looking back now, you simply cannot overstate the praise for Wilkinson and what he has done for a club which was in the very depths of depression when he took over. He has achieved all he set out to achieve but he has done it well ahead of schedule. Not once over the past three and a half years did his nerve threaten to desert him. His self-belief in the team which he built was unshakeable.

"It would be pointless to go through the current Leeds United side and list those players who have made important and significant contributions to a remarkable story of transformation and revival because there are so many.

"Gordon Strachan will continue to be a major influence, both on and off the field of play, for as long as he can steer clear of serious injury; Lee Chapman, much-maligned footballer that he is, will continue to score goal after goal for just so long as his midfield colleagues continue to supply him with half-chances, and the vastly under-rated defensive partnership of Chris Whyte and Chris Fairclough will, I am certain, go from strength to strength in the years ahead. They are a formidable team indeed.

"Like many of my journalistic colleagues, I have to say that I thought Leeds' chances of winning the title had evaporated when they were beaten by Manchester City at Maine Road. I just couldn't see them coming back from such a demoralising reversal. However, funny though it may seem, that defeat may have actually helped them more than they realise because it will have released a lot of the pressure which they were feeling. They certainly played with a good deal more fluidity in the games which were to follow.

"In contrast, at the precise moment Leeds were begin-ning to relax, Manchester United started to get a little hot under the collar as the weight of public expectation began to take a very heavy toll on players who felt duty-bound to win the Championship.

"Wilkinson's real master-stroke came after he had watched his side defeat Coventry City at Elland Road on Easter Monday. Although the result, when coupled with Manchester United's defeat by Nottingham Forest ear-lier in the day, took Leeds back to the top of the table, he hardly mentioned that fact in his press conference afterwards.

"All he kept stressing was that his team had reached its target by ensuring qualification for the UEFA Cup. He praised them to the heavens without once mentioning the Championship. That must have been a real boost for players who were beginning to show the first signs of battle-fatigue. They must have felt totally refreshed and free from pressure. It was a hugely successful uppercut in the prolonged psychological war which had been raging between Wilkinson and Alex Ferguson.

"I think that it is important that special mention is made of the role played by Leslie Silver, the Leeds chairman. He gave his manager unstinting support when it was needed – and hard cash when that was needed.

"Leeds United are very worthy Champions indeed but they should remember that winning the title is one thing, successfully defending it is another."

Most influential player? "**Gary McAllister.** A very difficult choice but he just shades it from Gary Speed who also enjoyed a fabulous season. McAllister is one of the most gifted, intelligent and productive midfield players in British football."

PHILIP McNULTY (*Liverpool Daily Post*): "I enjoyed watching Leeds United a great deal even if they were often to be found turning over one of the two Merseyside clubs. I was particularly impressed by what I saw on the day they defeated Liverpool at Elland Road.

"In beating Everton in the Rumbelows Cup at Goodison Park they produced a simply marvellous display of attacking football; one of the most memorable performances of the entire season.

"They have very many players of genuine quality and I suspect they will be a force to be reckoned with for several seasons.

"In the final count they won the Championship because they had a better manager than Manchester United – one who wasn't constantly meddling with his team. It might sound simple but I believe it made all the difference."

Most influential player? "**John Lukic.** This man has now won two League Championship medals with two different clubs and you do not do that unless you are exceptionally talented and extremely consistent."

DAVID MEEK (*Manchester Evening News*): "I do believe that Leeds United deserved to win the Championship if only because they managed to hold their nerve in those final, anxious few weeks when anything at all could have happened.

"I think that Howard Wilkinson proved himself to be a top-class manager by leading his side by example throughout the whole campaign. His influence was particularly noticeable towards the end when both Leeds and Manchester United started to wobble. At one stage it looked as though both sides would not only wobble but fall over. It was at that point that Wilkinson was successful in steadying his team and safely plotting a path through seas which were becoming increasingly turbulent.

"I have to agree with Alex Ferguson when he says that Leeds deserve full credit for their achievement. It is totally wrong for people to suggest that the First Division is somehow sub-standard because winning the League Championship is still arguably the most difficult task in European football.

"I don't really understand how these so-called experts can look back to the late Seventies and Eighties, when Liverpool were the dominant force in English football, and say that things were so much better then. One exceptional team does not necessarily make for a strong First Division. I enjoyed the season a great deal if only because it was far more open than of late. It seemed that any side which proved itself to be capable of stringing together an impressive sequence of results genuinely had a chance of taking the title.

"I have great admiration for Wilkinson because he is a man who cuts his coat according to the cloth which he has available to him. Having built a powerful side to win promotion from the Second Division he did well to modify it to suit football at the very highest level. His team is both attractive to watch and very well balanced."

Most influential player? "**Lee Chapman.** I think that it was his goals which made all the difference in the final count. For a man who has been banging in the goals for many, many years, Lee still has his detractors; people who still insist that he is some kind of a joke. Some joke!

"Although Brian McClair scored many valuable goals for Manchester United, the fact that their forwards did not hit the target as often as they should have done was probably the decisive factor.

"Lee Chapman was one of the most astute signings Howard Wilkinson will ever make."

PHIL SHAW (*The Independent*): "I must declare an interest here because I was born and bred in Leeds and saw my first game at Elland Road way back in 1959. To be honest, the fact that I have followed the club for so many years often makes me over-critical when called upon to cover their matches. I tend to find myself taking a supporter's point of view; they have to do much to please me. Having willingly declared this allegiance, it is important to add that if you can show me a football reporter who does not have a favourite team I will show you a liar.

"Before the start of the season, I did feel reasonably optimistic about Leeds' chances of doing well because I felt that Howard Wilkinson had spent his money wisely and invested in players of skill, potential and quality. In the previous season, I felt that Leeds definitely lacked pace which perhaps wasn't too surprising as several key members of the side were the wrong side of 30.

"I felt they needed an injection of pace and quality down the left, an area which had proved to be very polished and productive during the Don Revie era with players like Terry Cooper, Eddie Gray and Norman Hunter.

"Before the League programme opened, I had a bet with two of my journalistic colleagues, both of whom were insistent that Manchester United would win the title. I didn't actually have to specify which club was going to prevent them from reaching this target but, in truth, I thought it would be Arsenal. I was confident that Leeds would repeat their marvellous feat of the previous season and finish in the top four but I did feel it was probably a little premature to start talking in terms of them actually winning the Championship.

"My answer to those people – and there are many – who say that Manchester United lost the title rather than Leeds winning it is simple: the season was about much, much more than the run-in. The statistics speak for themselves on this occasion. Leeds lost only one League game in the first half of the season and only three in the second half when they suffered just as many injury problems as their nearest rivals. You can't knock the club's achievement in that respect.

"Who is to say whether or not Leeds United were the best team? Over the season they fully deserved to be Champions because they kept at it and never once threatened to buckle under the mental and physical pressure. It is strange that so many feel inclined to dismiss Leeds' achievement because if you reflect on the season they did produce several performances of genuine Championship quality. I am thinking particularly of the victories over Aston Villa at Villa Park and over Sheffield Wednesday at Hillsborough. In the end it was their sheer resilience and will to win which was to finally break the spirit of Manchester United.

"The attitude of the two managers, Wilkinson and Alex Ferguson, also had a lot to do with deciding the final outcome. Ferguson transparently felt the pressure, ironically, in much the same way as Don Revie used to do. Wilkinson, on the other hand, never seemed to let anything get to him; he always seemed to be in total control of the situation.

"There have been several other plus points this season. The arrival of Eric Cantona provided the supporters with a real cult hero and his extra flair could come in very useful next season when Leeds attempt to win the European Cup. Although the pace of English football does still seem to be a little too much for him, there is no one better equipped to come on, late in a game, and exploit a tiring defence. The emergence of Jon Newsome as a more than competent defender is another real bonus.

"Inevitably, there will be new talent introduced during the months which lie ahead. Howard Wilkinson will not let sentiment cloud his judgement and while I think he will give his Championship-winning team every opportunity to hold down their places, I do believe there will be several new faces by the time Leeds embark on their European campaign."

Most influential player? "**Gary McAllister.** His all-round game embraces accurate passing, great vision and tenacious tackling. His combination with David Batty at the heart of the Leeds midfield is very impressive and so valuable. I would give honourable mentions to Gary Speed and Tony Dorigo because they both enjoyed splendid seasons."

ALAN GREEN (Senior football commentator, BBC Radio Five): "It really is quite phenomenal what Leeds United have achieved under the managership of Howard Wilkinson in what is, in footballing terms, a very short period of time.

"The biggest compliment which I can pay the current Leeds team is to say that, in one respect at least, they remind me very much of Liverpool. That is, they may not always play particularly well but they have developed the knack – the habit – of picking up crucial points when they most need them. Several times I saw them squeeze out two extra points when they were below par. This is something which Liverpool have perfected down the years and something which is a vitally important asset for any side which has designs on winning the League Championship. Leeds didn't always look like Champions in the making but, to their immense credit, they stuck at the task even when people were writing them off on an almost daily basis.

"I must confess that before the season opened I didn't see them as likely winners of the title although I felt they would prove to be capable of equalling their achievement of the previous season when they finished in fourth place. I was full of admiration for the manner in which Wilkinson had set about the job of strengthening his senior squad but I thought they might just lack a little consistency when laid alongside teams like Liverpool, Arsenal and Manchester United.

"If I am totally honest, I would have to say that I believe their cause was definitely helped by the fact that this was a largely indistinguished year for English football at the very top level. I do believe that the First Division was a little ordinary. However, I am not, in any way, seeking to lessen Leeds' achievement because they are worthy Champions and along the way they produced some magnificent performances, particularly at Elland Road.

"It would have been very interesting to see what would have happened had the defending Champions, Arsenal, started their good run of form a little earlier. Had they hit their peak, say, two or three weeks earlier than they did, it could have been a lot tighter than it was at the top of the table come the end of April.

"Having said that, Wilkinson did a wonderful job of not only motivating his players but also keeping them away from the pressure. He is a manager who always talks a great deal of sense as far as I am concerned. It was constantly put to him that the First Division was not quite as strong as in previous years but this never once seemed to annoy him. He just kept repeating that there were still 42 games to play and that all his team could do was 'win it'.

"The same suggestion was also put to Alex Ferguson on a regular basis but it seemed to bother him a great deal more. He tended to bristle with anger whenever anyone sought to undermine his team's achievements.

"Wilkinson impressed me a great deal throughout the campaign, especially towards the end when he put his faith in those tried and trusted members of his team even though things weren't going too well. He guided them magnificently and he thoroughly deserved to pick up the Barclay's Manager of the Year award.

"Obviously, the fact that Leeds were eliminated from the two major cup competitions at a very early stage did help their cause because it left them free to focus all their attention on the one remaining prize. In the end, I suspect that Manchester United must have regretted the fact that their efforts were split between the League and the Rumbelows Cup. That may well have proved to be the decisive factor.

"I think, perhaps, the Leeds team has been underrated by the media because they do have several outstanding individuals. John Lukic is arguably the best goalkeeper in the First Division, Tony Dorigo was tremendous all season and the defensive partnership of Chris Whyte and Chris Fairclough was not only superb but crucial.

"Then, of course, there is Eric Cantona. What can you say about this lad? In terms of goals, the highlight of my whole season was his brilliant strike against Chelsea at Elland Road. You really would have to travel a long way to see a better goal than that one. Although I still have to be convinced that he has what it takes to make a lasting impression within the ultra-competitive world of English football, I thought Wilkinson used him brilliantly towards the end. He is the perfect man to throw on in the last 20 minutes when opposition defenders are beginning to slow down.

"I think that Manchester United undoubtedly had the best collection of players in the First Division but that Leeds United were the best unit, the best all-round team, and in the final count it is teamwork which wins titles."

Most influential player? "**Gary McAllister.** If I could pick a section, rather than an individual, then it would be the Leeds midfield which was so productive and very consistent. McAllister was the pivot of that midfield and he oozed class all through the season."

JOHN KEITH (*Daily Express*): "It really is stupid – and pointless – for people to turn around and say that Leeds' success is, in some way, second-class because the quality of the First Division is not what it was.

"The argument that teams were better and the football of a higher quality 20 years ago just doesn't hold water because you can make those sort of comparisons constantly, such is the transient nature of sport. As Howard Wilkinson said on so many occasions, his team could only win the division which they were in – and they did just that. Even Alex Ferguson, in what was his most depressing hour, was anxious that no one should devalue Leeds' achievement. After he had watched his side defeated by Liverpool at Anfield, he said that it would be totally unfair to suggest that the First Division was, in any way, mediocre. He was brave to do that but he was right.

"I don't think that very many people actually expected Leeds to win the Championship even though they had equipped themselves so well during the course of the previous season. It has been suggested that Manchester United handed the title to them in those last few weeks but the Championship is won over the course of a long and demanding season. I do believe that there is every chance that Leeds will now go from strength to strength.

"I say that because they have an astute manager who seems to have a gift for modifying his team to suit particular demands. If the target changes then Howard Wilkinson seems to be able to alter the make-up of his team to meet the extra demands.

"I think that the combination of Lee Chapman and Eric Cantona – the physical and the artistic – could prove to be very well suited to European football next season."

Most influential player? "**John Lukic.** Very few sides have won the League Championship with a mediocre goalkeeper. I have always admired Lukic and I just couldn't believe it when Arsenal allowed him to leave Highbury. I am surprised that he has not forced his way into the England national side."

Chapter Twelve

THE WAY FORWARD

Irrespective of what level of success is achieved by a football club, the days and weeks which follow memorable, perhaps even historic, events are invariably tinged with a measure of self-doubt. By their very nature, supporters are an impatient breed, willing to fall back on the age-old maxim – live for the moment – only for so long as it takes them to hungrily devour next season's fixture list. While it is, perhaps, understandable that those who willingly hand over their hard-earned money to fête their sporting heroes should steadfastly refuse to rest on their laurels, this undercurrent of grand expectation can present a multitude of problems for footballers who, having scaled the highest peak, suddenly find themselves back at base-camp confronted by a host of eager pretenders.

As anyone within the game will tell you, football is a sport which has almost been designed to ensure that triumph is followed by anti-climax. As anyone who has played in a successful team will tell you, winning the First Division Championship is one thing – retaining it is another. Not since Liverpool won the title in three consecutive seasons between 1981 and 1984 has a club managed to defend the most coveted prize in domestic football.

So what price Leeds United to succeed where the likes of Everton and Arsenal have failed?

Few would argue against the notion that the omens do look promising. Fewer still would be bold enough to suggest that Wilkinson's side has all the hallmarks of the proverbial one-season wonder.

Although chairman Leslie Silver is the first to acknowledge the severity of a task which now faces a team which is still relatively inexperienced in many respects, he is, typically, optimistic about both the immediate and long-term future of a club which continues to hold a curious fascination for him.

"I love Leeds United Football Club; it is a major part of my life and attempting to ensure its continued success is right at the very top of my priority list," he says with almost paternal affection. "Although I want the best for this club, and I want us to win everything we possibly can in the years ahead, I am a realist. I know full well that it will simply not be possible for us to win the biggest prize of all – the League Championship – each, and every, season. That is a lovely thought but it just couldn't happen.

"First and foremost what we must try and do is maintain the momentum which we have managed to build up over the past two or three years. If we can build a rock-solid base – a reliable foundation – then we can move forward with great confidence.

"It will surprise no one to learn that I would dearly love this club to progress along the lines of our old rivals, Liverpool. Over the past 25 years they have proved themselves to be an absolute model of consistency. They have shown just what can be achieved if a football club is structured properly and run properly. I am not saying that we will succeed in our attempts to emulate Liverpool but we can try; we must try."

While Silver is the very personification of sporting optimism, even he has been surprised, albeit pleasantly surprised, by the strength of the wind of change which has whistled through Elland Road's corridors of power since the arrival of Howard Wilkinson.

"Winning promotion back into the First Division at the end of the 1989-1990 season was the first landmark. After so many years in the Second Division the first feeling was one of sheer relief that we were finally back where I felt we always belonged. The first season after promotion can be difficult but we did marvellously well to finish in fourth place. I was delighted.

"To be perfectly honest, our aim was to try and launch a serious bid for the Championship, not this season, but next. Back in August I felt that winning a place in the UEFA Cup was an attainable target and one which we might achieve if all was to go well out on the field of play. It might be difficult to believe but Howard Wilkinson and myself never once discussed the possibility of us winning the title during the course of the season.

"Yes, we met regularly and often to talk about the way things were going and how improvements could be made but I saw our target as re-establishing ourselves as a top First Division club – one with the potential to win trophies at some point."

So, just four years after their ambition had embraced nothing more adventurous, nothing more enticing, than Second Division survival, the modern Leeds United will next season attempt to win the European Cup, something that was always to elude Don Revie's famous side of the Seventies.

"Don Revie was a great manager, of that there is no doubt at all. Now that we have again achieved success it is inevitable that people should be making comparisons between him and Howard Wilkinson or between his team and the present team. I think it is virtually impossible to do that because style and attitudes have changed so very much with the passing of the years.

"Don Revie's achievement was to make Leeds United not only a great and successful club but also a household name. Howard Wilkinson's achievement has been to re-establish this club and point it towards a new, brighter, horizon. Our intent now is to try and bring the European Cup to West Yorkshire for the very first time. I do believe that it is possible," said Silver.

Although Silver's sense of joy and satisfaction is, at present, uncontained, the fear that his manager, the man behind a remarkable transformation, may one day be courted by the Football Association as a successor to Graham Taylor, the England national manager, does serve to slightly temper his contentment.

"Because of what he has achieved in such a short space of time at this club, and because he led this club to the Championship against all expectations, Howard is, as they say, hot property within football at the moment. However, he does have a rolling contract with us which will carry him forward into the next century and I do hope that he is here for many more years. Quite simply, we do not want to lose him – not even to England."

Silver sees the development of Elland Road into a modern high-tec stadium with few equals as another obtainable goal in the years ahead. "As everyone knows, work on transforming our East Stand – the Lowfield Road Stand – will begin in the summer. It is a big and expensive job but when the work is completed in about 12 months time, we will have, what I am assured, will be the biggest span cantilever stand in Europe.

"After that our plans for ground improvements will centre around the Kop. To comply with Lord Justice Taylor's report, and to make Elland Road into an all-seater stadium, we shall be seating that section of the ground. Hopefully, everything will have been completed before the start of the 1994-95 season. The end product will be a comfortable, all-seater stadium which can house 40,000 people.

"We simply had to do everything we could to improve the ground's capacity because we couldn't guarantee admittance to everyone who wanted to attend our games. Very few clubs in this country can say that but, happily, we can.

"If people do want to come along and watch Leeds United then we have to ensure that we are in a position to cater for them. Because our capacity was reduced to just 29,000 in the wake of the Hillsborough disaster, I would estimate that we lost something like £750,000 just in gate receipts during our Second Division Championship-winning season.

"The other aspect is that we want our supporters to have the best possible facilities; we want the best team in the country and the best stadium. I think that it is important that we attempt to add something to the cultural approach of Leeds as a city. I want Elland Road to be a multi-complex stadium which is capable of staging not just top-quality football matches but also other leading events.

"In many respects we are very fortunate at this club. The actual situation of our ground is very advantageous because a great many English clubs are located within areas of concentrated population which quite obviously restricts their potential for growth and expansion. Elland Road really could not be better located, laying as it does at the heart of the motorway network and away from the city centre.

"I do believe that if this club can continue to grow and can continue to achieve a satisfactory level of success, it can also continue to prosper. Leeds, as a city, is unusual in that it has an enormous population yet has just the one football team. Most of the other large cities in the country – London, Birmingham, Liverpool, Manchester, Sheffield – have at least two Football League clubs fighting for support. If we can get things right out on the pitch and in terms of the stadium itself, I believe that we can attract average crowds of around 35,000."

Date	Opponents	F-A	Att	Pos	1	2	3	4	5	6	7	8	9	10	11	Sub	Sub
Aug 20	Nottingham Forest	H 1-0	29,457	-	Lukic	McClelland	Dorigo	Batty	Fairclough	Whyte	Strachan	Rod Wallace	Chapman	McAllister[1]	Speed	Sterland	Hodge
Aug 24	Sheffield Wednesday	H 1-1	30,260	10	Lukic	McClelland	Dorigo	Batty	Fairclough	Whyte	Strachan	Rod Wallace	Chapman	McAllister	Speed	Hodge (11)[1]	Sterland(2)[1]
Aug 28	Southampton	A 4-0	15,862	4	Lukic	McClelland	Dorigo	Batty	Fairclough	Whyte	Strachan[2]	Rod Wallace	Chapman	McAllister	Speed[2]	Sterland(5)	Hodge(10)
Aug 31	Manchester United	A 1-1	43,778	6	Lukic	Sterland	Dorigo	Batty	McClelland	Whyte	Strachan	Rod Wallace	Chapman[1]	McAllister	Speed	Hodge 10	Wetherall
Sep 3	Arsenal	H 2-2	29,396	6	Lukic	Sterland	Dorigo	Batty	McClelland	Whyte	Strachan	Rod Wallace	Chapman[1]	McAllister	Speed	Hodge (2)	Wetherall(3)
Sep 7	Manchester City	H 3-0	29,986	4	Lukic	Sterland	Dorigo[1]	Batty[1]	McClelland	Whyte	Strachan[1]	Rod Wallace	Chapman	McAllister	Speed	Hodge (8)	Wetherall
Sep 14	Chelsea	A 1-0	23,439	2	Lukic	Sterland	Dorigo	Batty	McClelland	Whyte	Strachan	Shutt[1]	Chapman	McAllister	Speed	Hodge (7)	Wetherall
Sep 18	Coventry City	A 0-0	15,488	2	Lukic	Sterland	Dorigo	Batty	McClelland	Whyte	Strachan	Shutt	Chapman	McAllister	Speed	Hodge (8)	Wetherall
Sep 21	Liverpool	H 1-0	32,917	2	Lukic	Sterland	Dorigo[1]	Batty	McClelland	Whyte	Strachan	Hodge[1]	Chapman	McAllister	Speed	Shutt (11)	Whitlow
Sep 28	Norwich City	A 2-2	15,828	2	Lukic	Sterland	Dorigo	Batty	Whyte	McClelland	Varadi	Hodge	Chapman	McAllister	Speed[1]	Shutt(7)	Whitlow(8)
Oct 1	Crystal Palace	A 0-1	18,298	2	Lukic	Sterland	Dorigo	Batty	McClelland	Whyte	Varadi	Hodge	Chapman	McAllister	Speed	Shutt(7)	Whitlow(10)
Oct 5	Sheffield United	H 4-3	28,362	2	Lukic	Sterland	Dorigo[1]	Batty	McClelland	Whyte	Hodge	Shutt	Chapman[1]	McAllister	Speed[1]	Fairclough (2)	Whitlow(10)
Oct 19	Notts County	A 4-2	12,964	2	Lukic	Sterland	Dorigo	Barry	Fairclough	Whyte	Strachan	Rod Wallace	Chapman[2]	Hodge[1]	Speed	McAllister(9)[1]	Kamara(12)
Oct 26	Oldham Athletic	H*1-0	28,199	1	Lukic	Sterland	Dorigo	Eatty	Fairclough	Whyte[1]	Strachan	Shutt	Chapman[1]	McAllister	Speed	Hodge[1]	Shutt(7)
Nov 2	Wimbledon	A 0-0	7,025	2	Lukic	Sterland	Dorigo	Shutt	Fairclough	Whyte	Strachan	Rod Wallace	Chapman	McAllister	Speed	Kamara(11)	Snodin
Nov 16	Queen's Park Rangers	H 2-0	27,087	1	Lukic	Sterland[1]	Dorigo	Batty	Fairclough	Whyte	Strachan	Rod Wallace[1]	Chapman	McAllister	Speed	Newsome(8)	McClelland
Nov 24	Aston Villa	A 4-1	23,713	1	Lukic	Sterland[1]	Dorigo	Batty	Fairclough	Whyte	Strachan	Rod Wallace[1]	Chapman[2]	McAllister	Speed	Varadi(11)	Hodge
Nov 30	Everton	H 1-0	30,043	1	Lukic	Sterland	Dorigo	Batty	Fairclough	Whyte	Strachan	Rod Wallace[1]	Chapman	McAllister	McClelland	Shutt	Hodge
Dec 7	Luton Town	A 2-0	11,550	1	Lukic	Sterland	Dorigo	Batty	Fairclough	Whyte	Strachan	Rod Wallace[1]	Chapman	McAllister	Speed[1]	Hodge(11)	McClelland(12)
Dec 14	Tottenham Hotspur	H 1-1	31,404	1	Lukic	Sterland	Dorigo	Batty	McClelland	Whyte	Strachan	Rod Wallace[1]	Chapman	McAllister	Speed[1]	Shutt	Hodge
Dec 22	Nottingham Forest	A 0-0	27,170	2	Lukic	Sterland	Dorigo	Batty	McClelland	Whyte	Strachan	Rod Wallace	Chapman	McAllister	Speed[1]	Kelly(7)	Hodge
Dec 26	Southampton	H 3-3	29,053	2	Lukic	Sterland	Dorigo[1]	Batty	McClelland	Whyte	Strachan	Rod Wallace	Chapman	McAllister	Speed	Kelly	Newsome
Dec 29	Manchester United	H 1-1	32,638	2	Lukic	Sterland[1]	Dorigo	Batty	McClelland	Whyte	Hodge[2]	Rod Wallace	Chapman	McAllister	Speed[1]	Hodge(4)	McClelland
Jan 1	West Ham United	A 3-1	21,766	1	Lukic	Sterland	Dorigo	Batty	Fairclough	Whyte	Strachan	Rod Wallace	Chapman	McAllister	Speed	Hodge(4)	McClelland
Jan 12	Sheffield Wednesday	A 6-1	32,228	1	Lukic	Sterland	Dorigo	Hodge	Fairclough	Whyte	Shutt	Rod Wallace	Chapman[2]	McAllister	Speed	Hodge	Shutt
Jan 18	Crystal Palace	H 1-1	27,717	1	Lukic	Sterland	Dorigo[1]	Batty	Fairclough[1]	Whyte	Strachan	Rod Wallace	Chapman[1]	McAllister	Speed	Whitlow(7)[1]	Davison(4)
Feb 1	Notts County	H 3-0	27,224	1	Lukic	Sterland[1]	Dorigo	Batty[1]	Fairclough	Whyte	Strachan	Rod Wallace[1]	Hodge	McAllister	Speed	Davison(10)	Whitlow(9)
Feb 8	Oldham Athletic	A 0-2	18,409	2	Lukic	Sterland	Dorigo	Batty	Fairclough	Whyte	Strachan	Rod Wallace	Hodge	McAllister	Speed	Cantona(9)	Whitlow(2)
Feb 23	Everton	A 1-1	19,248	2	Lukic	Sterland	Dorigo	Batty	Fairclough	Whyte	Strachan	Rod Wallace	Cantona	McAllister	Speed	Shutt(8)[1]	McClelland

Date	Opponent	Round	H/A	Score	Att.	Pos	1	2	3	4	5	6	7	8	9	10	11	Sub	Sub
Feb 29	Luton Town		H	2-0	28,231	2	Lukic	Sterland	Dorigo	Batty	Fairclough	Whyte	Strachan	Rod Wallace	**Chapman'**	McAllister	Speed	**Cantona(3)'**	Agana(8)
Mar 3	Aston Villa		H	0-0	28,896	2	Lukic	Sterland	Whitlow	Batty	Fairclough	Whyte	Strachan	Rod Wallace	Chapman	McAllister	Speed	McClelland(5)	Cantona(8)
Mar 7	Tottenham Hotspur		A	3-1	27,622	1	Lukic	Sterland	Whitlow	Batty	Fairclough	Whyte	Strachan	**Rod Wallace'**	Chapman	**McAllister'**	Speed	**Newsome(2)'**	Cantona(3)
Mar 11	Queen's Park Rangers		A	1-4	14,641	1	Lukic	Newsome	Whitlow	Batty	Fairclough	Whyte	Strachan	**Rod Wallace'**	**Chapman'**	McAllister	**Speed'**	Cantona(10)	Grayson
Mar 14	Wimbledon		A	5-1	26,760	1	Lukic	Newsome	**Cantona'**	Batty	Fairclough	Whyte	Strachan	**Rod Wallace'**	**Chapman²**	McAllister	Speed	Shutt(7)	Mauchlen
Mar 22	Arsenal		A	1-1	27,844	1	Lukic	Cantona	Dorigo	Batty	Fairclough	Whyte	Strachan	Rod Wallace	**Chapman'**	McAllister	Speed	Newsome	Hodge
Mar 28	West Ham Utd		H	0-0	31,101	1	Lukic	Cantona	Dorigo	Batty	Fairclough	Newsome	Strachan	Rod Wallace	Chapman	McAllister	Speed	Hodge(8)	Mauchlen
Apr 4	Manchester City		A	0-4	30,239	2	Lukic	Cantona	Dorigo	Batty	Fairclough	Whyte	Strachan	Rod Wallace	**Chapman'**	McAllister	Speed	Newsome	Hodge
Apr 11	Chelsea		H	3-0	31,363	1	Lukic	Hodge	Dorigo	Batty	Fairclough	Whyte	Strachan	**Rod Wallace'**	**Chapman'**	McAllister	Speed	Newsome(2)	**Cantona(8)'**
Apr 18	Liverpool		A	0-0	37,186	2	Lukic	Newsome	Dorigo	Batty	Fairclough	Whyte	Hodge	Rod Wallace	Chapman	McAllister	Speed	Cantona(7)	McClelland
Apr 20	Coventry City		H	2-0	26,582	1	Lukic	Newsome	Dorigo	Batty	**Fairclough'**	Whyte	Strachan	**Rod Wallace'**	Chapman	**McAllister'**	Speed	Cantona(8)	Shutt(7)
Apr 26	Sheffield United		A	3-2	32,000	1	Lukic	**Newsome'**	Dorigo	Batty	Fairclough	Whyte	Strachan	**Rod Wallace'**	Chapman	McAllister	Speed	Shutt(7)	Cantona(10)
May 2	Norwich City		H	1-0	32,673	1	Lukic	Newsome	Dorigo	Batty	Fairclough	Whyte	Cantona	**Rod Wallace'**	Chapman	McAllister	Speed	Strachan(9)	Hodge(7)

ZENITH DATA SYSTEMS CUP

Date	Opponent	Round	H/A	Score	Att.	Pos	1	2	3	4	5	6	7	8	9	10	11	Sub	Sub
Oct 22	Nottingham Forest	R2	H	1-3	6,495	-	Lukic	Sterland	Dorigo	Batty	Fairclough	Whyte	Newsome	Shutt	Snodin	Kamara	Speed	**Rod Wallace(2)'**	Grayson(7)

RUMBELOWS LEAGUE CUP

Date	Opponent	Round	H/A	Score	Att.	Pos	1	2	3	4	5	6	7	8	9	10	11	Sub	Sub
Sep 24	Scunthorpe Utd.	R2-1L	A	0-0	8,392	-	Lukic	Sterland	Dorigo	Batty	McClelland	Whyte	Strachan	Hodge	Chapman	McAllister	Speed	Shutt(7)	Whitlow
Oct 8	Scunthorpe Utd.	R2-2L	H	3-0	14,558	-	Lukic	**Sterland'**	Dorigo	Batty	McClelland	Whyte	Hodge	Shutt	**Chapman'**	Williams	**Speed'**	Fairclough(10)	Kelly(8)
Oct 29	Tranmere Rovers	R3	H	3-1	18,266	-	Lukic	Sterland	Dorigo	Hodge	Fairclough	Whyte	Strachan	**Shutt'**	**Chapman²**	McAllister	Rod Wallace	Kamara(4)	Williams(11)
Dec 4	Everton	R4	A	4-1	25,467	-	Lukic	Sterland	Dorigo	Batty	Fairclough	Whyte	Strachan	**Rod Wallace²**	**Chapman'**	McAllister	**Speed'**	Hodge(7)	McClelland
Jan 8	Manchester United	R5	H	1-3	28,886	-	Lukic	Sterland	Dorigo	Batty	Fairclough	Whyte	Strachan	Rod Wallace	Chapman	McAllister	**Speed'**	McClelland(3)	Hodge(9)

FA CUP

Date	Opponent	Round	H/A	Score	Att.	Pos	1	2	3	4	5	6	7	8	9	10	11	Sub	Sub
Jan 15	Manchester United	R3	H	0-1	31,819	-	Lukic	Sterland	Dorigo	Hodge	Fairclough	Whyte	Williams	Wallace	Chapman	McAllister	Speed	Davison (4)	Whitlow (7)

Players name in **bold** type denote goalscorers. Figures in brackets after the substitutes name indicate the player replaced. *Denotes Own Goal.